Cosmic Consciousness
One Man's Search for God

by Mark L. Prophet *as recorded by*
Elizabeth Clare Prophet

"What man has done, man can do."
—Mark L. Prophet

SUMMIT UNIVERSITY ☽ PRESS®

To the Darjeeling Master
and his followers

Cosmic Consciousness
One Man's Search for God
by Mark L. Prophet
as recorded by Elizabeth Clare Prophet

Library of Congress Catalog Card Number: 74-24023
International Standard Book Number: 0-916766-17-9

This book is set in 12 point Elegante with 1 point lead.
Printed in the United States of America
First Printing: 1976. Second Printing: 1977. Third Printing: 1981
Fourth Printing: 1983. Fifth Printing: 1986. Sixth Printing: 1987

For information on the magnificent art of Nicholas Roerich,
write Nicholas Roerich Museum, 319 West 107th St.,
New York, NY 10025.

Cover: Taken from a painting by Nicholas Roerich,
Mohammed upon Mount Hira.

SUMMIT UNIVERSITY ⍦ PRESS®

Mark L. Prophet walked before us as a friend on the Path. "Seized with a passion that is the love of God," Mark illustrated Truth as a day-to-day experience of God that could come to all. For him, the path of Truth led to cosmic consciousness.

He won because he never stopped loving people—all kinds of people. And he never lost patience with seeing through to the end the needs of his friends. He was equally enduring with strangers and even the self-styled enemies that everyone who truly loves encounters on life's way.

While showing a rare tenderness and deep sensitivity to his students' innermost needs, he was well known for his instant intolerance toward the assailants of the soul's upward striving—those assassins of one's own highest virtues that from time to time rise up from the mists of the subconscious.

Master psychologist—for he read the soul and heart of a man as no other could—fearless defender of the integrity of the individual, lover of Christ and feeder of his sheep, this giant of a man was never so tall as to not bend to the lowliest among us and lift up that one as a babe in arms to the point of self-recognition in God.

"Because Thou art, O God, I AM!" was his mantra of be-ness, and he affirmed it for all until they, no longer content to walk in his shadow, would follow the path of personal God-realization to the Sun.

Yes, he endured his own imperfections as Paul did before him, who was never without his "thorn in the flesh," as he put it. But God in him was greater than all of that. In him we saw the timeless ritual of the Lord's sweeping down upon his anointed, raising him up for an holy purpose, and, in the very process, the Son of God transcending the son of man.

Sometimes we looked at him as though he were a god—because of our own weakness—and then we saw him all too much a man, as though we ourselves were gods. Such poor perspective is the plight of our human minds.

But we listened to his Voice. We knew it well. Blindfolded, we would have followed it over the hills to the highway's end.

Then one day the Prophet spoke to us no more and his voice became the echo of conscience in our souls. Now there is a special chamber in our hearts where we go to hear him sing to us anew his lullaby of the AUM. There we remember that once we beheld a shaft of light swing through our space, beheld the man transparent for its grace, beheld the eyes compelling us to climb the highest mountain where we too might see God face to face. There we remember how we watched as the shaft swung back again carrying him to other shores.

But for you, dear friend, he left footprints—big and well outlined—of his path of practical "Christ-I AM-ity," as he loved to call the Way of his dear Saviour.

Simple yet profound, serious to the nth and suddenly laughable by sheer buffoonery as in self-mockery, he would teach us the cardinal rule of life—"Don't take yourself too seriously. Don't be seized with your own self-importance."

Disarming, as in the role of pure fool he would, with rapier thrust worthy of Launcelot, thrust home to our souls the piercing wisdom that laid bare the phantom of personal pride and our most sacred, secret sins. And suddenly we would be as free as he, uninhibited, little-boy-and-girlish—embarrassed by our supercilious egos and so glad he had dismissed the specters of our yesterdays before anyone saw just how nonsensical those ancestral idols were—the ones that followed us all pious in their superfluity, that is, until he began to speak.

And so by relentless holiness this divine comédien—who would first disarm the carnal mind and then summarily bind the beasts that preyed upon our innocence—this twentieth-century adept let us know that it's okay to be human as long as you remember you're divine. But if you think you're all divine, you're probably too divine to be human. And after all, it's in our very humanness that we can afford to love and win!

ELIZABETH CLARE PROPHET

Contents

To feel love is to desire
to be that love.
And to be that love
is to continually transcend
the former state until
heaven is realized on earth.

The Message
of the Master
upon the Ascension
of the Disciple

Ascension/Celebration

for your initiation on the path of the Heart ☉

foreword

*The Son of Man
shall come
again
with Healing
in his wings...*

...to unleash
the lightning
of
Creativity
Sublime.

To Those Who Look Upward
to Behold the Son of Man,

The disciples who beheld the
ascension of Jesus were accosted
by two men who stood by them
in white apparel and said,
"Ye men of Galilee, why stand ye
gazing up into heaven?

"This same Jesus, which is
taken up from you into heaven,
shall so come in like manner as ye
have seen him go into heaven."[1]

And so upon the occasion of
the ascension of our messenger
Mark L. Prophet, I say to each and
every one of you that when a son of
God returns to the heart of God

through the ritual of the ascension,
by the law of cycles he must also
return to the field of battle
and to the world whence he came
and over which he achieved the
victory—there to bring the glad
tidings of the light of victory
to all who walked with him on
the homeward path.

Jesus' promise to his disciples
who would believe upon him was
the accomplishment of greater works
"because I go unto my Father."[2]

Understand the law and be
satisfied thereby.

The Light which lighteth every
man that cometh into the world[3]
is the Light that he must expand
through the flame within the
heart in order to achieve that
glorious reunion of the soul with
the Spirit that is known as the
marriage of the Lamb.[4]

I say then to you, one and all—
those who grieve the loss of a dear
friend and teacher and those of you
who are able to rejoice in his
glorious attainment—that because he
has gone to the Father, he can add
the momentum of his causal body
to your own, that you also might do

those greater works which were
promised to the disciples of Jesus.

Each time a son or a daughter
of God ascends, those who are
ready to receive it are blessed by
the presence of the Holy Spirit,
the descent of the Paraclete.
And the communion cup of
hierarchy is shared once again with
the children of God who yet dwell
in the valley of becoming.

The parting words of the avatar
to those who gather round to
receive the mantle of his victory
must always be "It is expedient
for you that I go away: for if
I go not away, the Comforter will
not come unto you; but if I depart,
I will send him unto you."[5]

Simultaneously, as the flame
that is man rises to become one
with the flame that is God, there is
showered upon those who understand
the law and who pursue its spirit,
the contents of the cup of the
Holy Grail.

The Comforter is the essence
of Life, of the Holy Spirit,
that fulfills the prayer of Jesus
"Father, make them one even as
we are one."[6]

I exhort you, O chelas of the will of God, to realize that the door to heaven stands wide open because your messenger and mine has opened it, not only for himself but for you and for all mankind.

If he had but given the last energies of his life to the teaching and to the publication thereof—aye, that would have been enough to open the door. But by earning his victory through dauntless service and unquenchable love for God and man, he paved the pathway before you that you, too, might ascend into the very Presence of God.

How can there be sadness upon earth when there is rejoicing in heaven? There is sadness because men consider themselves to be alone and do not realize that aloneness is *all-one-ness.*

Never before in this embodiment have you had such an opportunity to pursue the flame, to feel its heat upon your brow and in your hand. For the cascading tides of Life from the heart of the God Presence, from the heart of every ascended master now flow into your world over the pathway that he has trod before you.

Mighty footprints in the sands
of life has our messenger left.
And all who are wise will seek
them out and place their feet in that
unmistakable, clearly marked
pathway which he has shown.

The glory of the Piscean age
initiated by Jesus was fulfilled in
him.

He walked the solitary path.
And he walked the path of union
with the hearts of all mankind.

He bore his brother's burden.
And he counted not the cost of
giving his all to all who came for
counsel, for comfort, for convincing
in the law.

As we sat at the Darjeeling
Council table last evening, I said to
Saint Germain: "What a triumph in
the midst of darkness! How our
light has shone! As the lightning
that cometh out of the East and
shineth even unto the West, so has
been the coming of this son of God
to the earth."[7]

And Saint Germain smiled at
me with a smile that encompassed
the whole world, and he said:
"I knew that he would fulfill the

plan. I knew that there was a man who would not fail our Cause. And standing by his side also, shrinking not from the battlefield of life, is the Mother chosen of old to nurture the children of mankind and a planet that yearns for the succor of the Divine Mother. You trained them well, my friend. And they have borne witness to the truth in this generation."

As Jesus spoke to the ruler of the Jews who came to him by night, so I say to you in the true spirit of the Christ: "That which is born of the flesh is flesh; and that which is born of the Spirit is spirit."[8]

The best way that I can convey to you the meaning of the ascension is to liken it unto the birth of a tiny babe into its fleshly form. For the ascension is the birth into the Spirit.

As man comes forth and bears the image of the earthy, so he returns to God to bear the image of the heavenly.[9] The ascension day of every man is the birthday of his immortal reunion with God—the day that commemorates the hour of victory when he becomes a pillar

(of fire) in the temple of God,
nevermore to go out into physical
form to bear the burden of the
sin of the world within his
four lower bodies.[10]

The wind bloweth where it listeth
And thou hearest the sound thereof
But canst not tell whence it cometh
And whither it goeth:
So is every one that is born
    of the Spirit.[11]

To be born of the Spirit
Is to be borne of the Spirit.
And so is every ascended being,
The company of saints,
The hosts that are camped
Upon the hillsides of the world.

Among them standing tall,
Clothed in robe of white
And sash of brilliant sapphire blue,
Is the messenger of the
    Great White Brotherhood
Who proclaims to you still
The message of the sacred Word,
The oft-repeated sound of harmonies,
Mantras, invocations spoken by angels
That come tumbling down the corridor
That echoes with a fateful sound:
I AM free, I AM free,
I AM free forevermore!

We are one, we are one,
We are one forevermore!
There is no death, no parting,
    no sorrow,
But all-oneness, all-oneness,
And tomorrow and tomorrow
    and tomorrow...

The crystal cord has risen
To carry a heart of fire
Back to its Source
While the blessed elementals,
Oromasis and Diana
Have taken that noble form
And returned it to the Eternal Bourn.
From Light to Light,
From Glory unto Glory,[12]
This is the word—
Not dust to dust![13]

For the Son of man shall come again
With healing in his wings[14]
To raise each heart and to impart
The comfort from on high
"I will not leave you comfortless:
I will come to you.
Yet a little while
And the world seeth me no more
But ye see me:
Because I live
Ye shall live also."[15]

The promise of the ages is fulfilled.
The promise that God willed,
The promise of man to God
And God to man,
Is the covenant instilled
In every heart and mind—
The stain of centuries to bind
And to unleash the lightning
Of creativity sublime!

The Brothers and Sisters of the Diamond Heart and the entire Darjeeling Council assembled salute you in the Spirit of the ascension flame.

We beckon you onward. And we offer it to you—a cup of light in His name.

May I introduce to you, then, the ascended master Lanello—to whom you may now call and whom you may address, knowing well that the friend whose hand you shook, whose smile greeted you once, will greet you again in the eternal embrace of Love's victory won.

I AM your mentor
on the Path,

El Morya

Behold!
I AM Everywhere
in the Consciousness
of God.

A New Dimension of Cosmic Awareness

Preparation/Edification

for your Capricorn initiation on the path of the Heart ♑

chapter one

*To prepare you
for the ritual
of the ascension
in the Light...*

*...through the
quickening fires
of the
World Mother.*

Heart Friends of the Light of Freedom,

I come to renew the ancient covenant, to surround you with the swaddling garment of my immortality, to enfold you in the spirals of my immortal awareness, to mesh my consciousness with your own.

My purpose is a many-faceted one. First and foremost, that which is on my heart is to prepare each and every one of you who have known me as Mark—who assisted me in my service to Life and who lended support to The Summit Lighthouse—for the ritual of the return known as the ascension in the light. For, having come so recently from the planes of Mater, being so aware of the stresses and strains attendant upon life in the decade of the seventies, I am in a unique position to assist you along the homeward way.

To those of you who have recently come into the fold of the ascended masters' teachings, who have heard the call of the Great White Brotherhood and who have responded to the flame of the Mother, I say: Greetings in the name of the risen Christ! Be thou made whole.

Welcome to our hearth and home!—to the Retreat of the Resurrection Spiral in Colorado Springs, to the Motherhouse in Santa Barbara, to the ascended masters' university. And, above all, welcome to the teachings of the ascended masters that have been preserved for you through our mission.

These will be released to you in the coming months in heightened measure as the messenger and the devoted staff move with the legions of Hercules and of the God Mercury to translate the spoken Word to the printed page for the victory of the light in the hearts of light-bearers the world around.

The Darjeeling Council of the Great White Brotherhood has asked me to prepare a series of Pearls of Wisdom for your edification and for the preparation and admonishment of your souls.

For hierarchy is concerned that the remnant of the sons and daughters of God upon the planet be energized with the new currents of the Aquarian cycle and of the golden age—that here and there across the planetary home, clusters of light-bearers gather for the intensification of the spirals of victory in these final hours of testing, of tribulation, and yes, of temptation.

We are determined by the grace of God to activate the consciousness of the Divine Feminine upon earth in individuals, in organizations, and in the most unexpected groups and societies. As you, then, respond to the quickening fires of the World Mother, you will also intensify the action of my flame, my being and consciousness, right within your very midst.

Even now I am merging the attainment of my Christ consciousness with your own beloved Holy Christ Self, that my consciousness, reinforcing that of your own Higher Mind, might provide the bridge whereby this mortal might put on immortality, this corruptible might put on incorruption.[1]

The translation of the soul from the planes of Mater to the planes of Spirit is accompanied by a liberating force, a solar light that eclipses all darkness—melting the elements of the subconscious with a fervent heat,[2] repolarizing the very atoms and molecules of being to the divine blueprint that is that perfection of the soul which is the true nature of being itself.

"There is a way that seemeth right unto a man, but the end thereof are the ways of death."[3]

There are many paths, many teachers and the proverbial guru who set themselves up in the midst of followers who earnestly seek the divine Light.

In some cases, these are the instruments of hierarchy preparing segments of the population to receive the greater effulgence of the Mother flame. In other cases, these self-styled teachers along the way provide detours and often capture their listeners in a cul-de-sac of consciousness where they remain, alas, sometimes for several incarnations.

I am determined, hierarchy is determined, by the grace of the Holy Spirit to so imbue those representatives of our holy cause who are coming forth from the ascended masters' university and from among the student body in the field with such light and purity and radiance so as to create a forcefield in the world that is a magnet for truth and for the wholeness of that truth which shall indeed make all mankind free.[4]

A partial truth is as dangerous as error itself. For it is the partial truths that beset orthodoxy in its many forms in East and West that effectively seal the earnest yet unenlightened seeker from the enlightenment of the Buddhic consciousness.

I come, then, to prepare the way for the universal acceptance of the offering of the Cosmic Christ in this age.

I come to prepare each of my readers with increasing increments of light with each release set forth herewith as a testimony of my witness to the truth in all ages.

I come to make you sun centers—to increase the decibels of consciousness to a new dimension of cosmic awareness.

And when the energies within heart and soul and mind blend for the release of the balanced action of the threefold flame, then you will see the explosion of light that occurs through the merging of the fires of Alpha and Omega right within you—right within your being, consciousness, and world.

By that explosion of the sacred fire, you will see the multiplication of the Lord's body, of the loaves and fishes that shall be for the feeding of the five thousand.[5]

You will see how your consecration, your unswerving

allegiance to Principle, will make of you a sun center with radiating light going forth to contact hundreds, thousands, and eventually millions who yearn to see the light of the new day but who, because of karmic ties and a dense stratification of consciousness, must await your own self-mastery ere they can move upward in the climb to summit heights.

Do you see, precious hearts, that hierarchy is a chain of being?

Hierarchy represents the highest and the lowest on the evolutionary chain. Somewhere along this chain of being is the link of your identity—your identity that is hid with Christ in God.[6]

This link in the chain of being makes you responsible for your actions. First, to Almighty God in the center of being, whose consciousness is also anchored in the center of every link in the chain. Second, you are responsible to the individual identity who occupies that place in hierarchy just above your own. And third, you are responsible to the individual who occupies the position just below your own.

To the one above you, you owe unswerving allegiance and a determination to defend the Christ principle at all costs. This one who is next in line in hierarchy above you may be your teacher in the plane of Mater, an unascended hierarch and member of the Great White Brotherhood—or it may be your Guru, an ascended master, the chohan of one of the seven rays.[7]

The identity immediately beneath you in this chain of being is the initiate on the path who is following in your footsteps, who receives the momentum of victory each time you pass an initiation and who is also overcome by your failure each time you miss an opportunity to express the wholeness of the Christ.

You are likewise responsible to all beings on the scale of God's consciousness beneath you in the long line of evolution. And, of course, you are responsible to all those who have preceded you—to keep the flame, to carry the torch of Life, and to pass on those frequencies of higher octaves to beings dwelling in lower octaves of evolution.

As you rise in self-mastery with greater attainment, greater ability to focus the light of God-control, God-harmony, and God-reality, you are rewarded with energy-increments of God-power until you become a veritable sun center.

And you know, one of the most important properties of the sun center is the central sun magnet—a forcefield in the white-fire core that magnetizes light for and on behalf of lifewaves and demagnetizes any focus or forcefield of all energies less than Light's perfection.

We come, then, to the place where the ascended masters of the Great White Brotherhood who comprise hierarchy in the realm of Spirit desire to mesh their consciousness in greater measure with unascended initiates of that brotherhood who desire to be representatives for and on behalf of the Light to a world waiting for the Second Coming of the Christ.

In order to implement that

manifestation, the Christ mind must be elevated in increasing numbers of devotees across the planetary home. For the day must shortly come to pass when mankind's teachers shall not "be removed into a corner anymore" but all shall see their teachers face to face.[8]

The beginning of the appearance of the ascended masters as it has been foretold to you, which will commence with the appearance of Mother Mary in the West, must come about first through the power of the spoken and the written Word, and then through the consciousness of the ascended masters merging with their unascended disciples.

Your daily recitation of the rosary[9] is a sacred ritual whereby the spirals of the Mother ray merge with your being and you walk the earth as Her representative.

As you put on, for example, the robe of Maitreya, the mantle of his consciousness and his attainment, you become the living, breathing awareness of the Cosmic Christ in manifestation.

As you are able to maintain

that attunement for greater periods in time and space, by your consecration you will be found as the forerunner, preparing the way for that day when the Cosmic Christ will step through the veil— giving first to the few and then to the many the interpretation of Scripture, the mysteries of the law, and the unfoldment of that wisdom which comes forth from the retreats of the Great White Brotherhood.

As you prepare to receive the releases of the ascended masters which will be forthcoming in the Pearls of Wisdom, I ask you with the full fervor of my being to concentrate your energies in the giving of decrees and invocations to the flame of the solar light—to purity, to freedom, and to the will of God (see p. 264).

In the words of Paul I say: "What? Know ye not that your body is the temple of the Holy Ghost which is in you, which ye have of God, and ye are not your own? For ye are bought with a price: therefore glorify God in your body, and in your spirit, which are God's."[10]

In the memory of our origin in immortal spheres, I embrace you with the love of my heart.

Lanello

The Balance of the Threefold Flame

Translation/Evolution

for your Aquarius initiation on the path of the Heart ♒

chapter two

A destiny preordained from the Beginning...

*... Freedom to choose
to Be
the manifold expression
of the
Threefold Flame of Life.*

Heart Flames Dedicated to the Balance
   of Love, Wisdom, and Power,

   When the Apostle Paul
declared your body to be the
temple of the Holy Ghost, he also
saw that the day would come when
many among mankind would be
raised up to be the instruments of
the Paraclete, quickened to deliver
to the age a mandate of the glory of
God incarnate.
   The age which he foresaw is
upon us. And the time of the
appearing of the Holy Ghost in man
and in woman draws nigh.
   As John the Baptist went forth
to prepare the way for the coming

of the Christ in Jesus, so I come to you in this hour in the power of the spoken Word to prepare the way for the coming of the Christ into full, balanced manifestation within you.

The balance of which I speak is the balance of the threefold flame, which is the spark of your Divinity that burns upon the altar of the heart.

This spark that is the threefold action of the love, wisdom, and power of the Father/Mother God is the sacred fire that burns on the altar of the temple of the Holy Ghost. It is the fire of Life which you must keep as a Keeper of the Flame. And when that fire is adored as the very living Presence of God himself, then and only then does your body become the actual dwelling place of the Holy Ghost.

In this the second week of our instruction on the putting on of the garment of the Lord, we concentrate upon the need for the students to prepare the body temple for the coming of the Holy Spirit. And we show you how you can present yourself a living sacrifice[1] on the altar of the Lord.

The threefold flame is the core of your identity. And around that core, the Father/Mother God has coalesced the energies which provide for your self-conscious awareness of God as Spirit and of soul as your living potential to become the fullness of God in manifestation.[2]

Jesus and others who have walked the homeward path have become the fullness of the Christ in outer manifestation by balancing the energies of the threefold flame within the heart.

In the beginning when you were created in the plane of Spirit, this flame was a Trinity of God's consciousness. But after the descent into form and the subsequent fall from levels of perfection through misuse and the misapplication of the gift of free will, the aspects of the threefold flame no longer manifested in balance.

With the loss of the balance of love, wisdom, and power came the loss of the Christ consciousness, which then receded to the level of mediator, acting as a go-between

between the imperfection of the outer evolving consciousness and the perfection of the great inner God Self.

The four lower bodies of mankind[3] no longer mirrored the fullness of Christ-love, Christ-wisdom, and Christ-power. And man forgot that his outer consciousness was but the instrument of the inner fire and the inner equation that was and is the threefold flame.

Thus the spark of Life that kept the flow of Life moving in the temple foursquare, while unbalanced in its manifestation in the world of material form, had a counterpart in the Holy Christ Self—the real identity of man and woman.

Within the heart of the Holy Christ Self, there remained the perfect outpicturing of the threefold flame as it was intended to one day come forth into manifestation in the body temple.

Now as we look to make of the devotees of the sacred fire among mankind instruments for the stepping through the veil of members of hierarchy, we must turn our attention to the giving of that needed instruction which can assist every soul to draw forth from the Holy Christ Self the balancing action of the threefold flame that will magnetize, even in the plane of Matter, the perfection of the Sacred Trinity.

Therefore, in the seven-day period in which you study this Pearl of Wisdom and apply its teaching, which comes to you at the behest of the Darjeeling Council, will you not meditate in equal measure upon the flame of love in the giving of self without reserve, upon the flame of wisdom in the application of the mind to the higher teaching of the law, and upon the flame of power through obedience to the covenants of our Maker?

And I ask that you make invocations to the Lords of Karma that there might be revealed to you those impediments which remain in your outer personality at subconscious as well as conscious levels which prevent the flow of a threefold flame in balanced action in your world.

When these conditions are revealed to you, you ought to follow the sacred ritual of writing them down in your own handwriting and then submitting them to Almighty God in the rite of true sacrifice whereby the supplicant places upon the altar of the sacred fire every aspect of himself which is unreal, hence unworthy of being perpetuated in the flame of Life.

This is that true sacrifice which must be practiced if the redemption of the Holy Ghost is to come upon the devotees in this age.

There is great significance in ritual. And the ritual of consigning to the flame those conditions of consciousness which are made known to the aspirant by the Higher Mind is one important means of stripping the outer self of its illusions.

This ritual leads to greater awareness of the True Self and enables the disciple to narrow the gap that presently exists between the outer evolving consciousness that is in the state of becoming the Christ and the full-orbed presence of that Christed One.

As this gap is narrowed through invocation and application to the sacred fire and through service to one's fellowman, the goal of oneness with Reality is approached and the possibility, ever present, of ultimate victory is more clearly at hand.

Our goal, then, in this series of Pearls of Wisdom is to draw the outer consciousness into greater alignment with the soul and the Christ Self, that man and woman in this age might walk the earth in the full, breathing awareness of the vitality of being sons and daughters of God in the highest sense—joint-heirs[4] of the Christ consciousness here and now!

Now I recommend for your study in conjunction with this dispensation a *Trilogy on the Threefold Flame of Life* written by my illustrious teacher and friend the ascended master Saint Germain. For indeed the key to self-mastery is the glorious fulfillment of light's Trinity—as above, so below.

For the glory of the sun and of the moon and of the stars of which

Saint Paul speaks[5] is this glory of the spark of Life, that precious seedling God has sown throughout the vastness of the Cosmic Egg as a focal point for the spiraling of Divinity into manifestation in form in the body of the Mother.

Paul speaks of celestial bodies and bodies terrestrial and the glory of the celestial as one and the glory of the terrestrial as another.[6]

So it is that there is a translation of energy: the same energy which manifests as Father in the plane of Spirit coalesces as Mother in the plane of Matter. And yet the glory and the radiance of this energy manifests according to the frequency of God's consciousness appearing as Life in these several dimensions of being.

The translation of the energies of Spirit to form—the womb of Mater with its manifold dimensions of time and space and levels of consciousness occupying this hallowed space you call your native universe—is but the accord of the Father/Mother God to provide opportunity for evolution for billions of lifestreams.

These streams of life are the individual identities which emanate from the Sun Source center of being, created by God to expand self-awareness of the Divine One.

All of life is God.

All of being is God.

All of consciousness is God. We come to understand him in his many facets as we understand the law of the translation of energy whereby God can identify himself as inert matter, as flaming flame of the one Life, as elemental, angelic being, cosmic hierarchy, even as he is the essence of the planes of fire, air, water, and earth in the body of the Mother.

There is, then, a translation of energy from Spirit to Matter, even as you observe in the passing of loved ones the translation of material energies to the plane of spiritual being.

Moving on the scale of the dimensions of Matter, mankind enter physical existence and depart therefrom—all the while yet remaining in the plane of Matter until evolution and self-mastery are complete, until that hour and that moment when there is the quickening of being for the final translation of the body of the Mother which merges with and becomes the Spirit of the Father.

This final translation is the return of the soul to the plane of Spirit in the ritual of the ascension.

We come to intensify. We come to magnify hearts yearning to be free—hearts yearning to prove the consciousness of God here in this body, to fire this body and be fired by the energies of the Holy Ghost, then to be made a permanent atom in the being of God and to return to those octaves where there is limitless opportunity for expansion in the timeless/ spaceless dimensions of Spirit.

"He must increase, but I must decrease"[7]—the words of John the Baptist referring to the tender regard in which he held the Master Jesus.

As mankind behold the creation and query within themselves as to the purposes of that creation, they must understand that it is the fire of the heart that must be increased in the plane of

Matter, and sin and the sense of sin in the separation of the outer self from the Source which must be decreased.

In direct proportion to the increase of the measure of the flame of Spirit that is anchored in the form will be the progress and the initiation of the disciple on the Path.

The threefold flame of Life vibrates at the level of Spirit. It is the focal point of God as Spirit in manifestation in man, whose soul in the present hour yet occupies a point of contact in time and space that is for the realization of God as Mother.

To make you one with us in all planes of being is the goal of our communication. And our love for evolving humanity is so great that if it were possible, we would lay down our very life for the salvation of all.

"Whosoever seeks to save his life shall lose it, and whosoever loses his life for my sake shall find it again."[8]

Thus we seek to enhance the life of God. Losing ourselves in service to untold billions, we find that as we nourish the fires of Divinity here below, so our life as God individualized in Spirit is increased here above.

As you hold the contact for hierarchy upon earth, we increase that contact in heaven.

And all of the evolutions of God—as above, so below—move forward in the cosmic spiral of a destiny that was preordained from the beginning. A destiny that is the freedom of the sons and daughters of God to choose to be the manifold expression of the threefold flame of Life.

I AM yours for the salvation of a planet and her people,

Lanello

A Dissertation on Death and Dying

Transition/Etherealization

for your Pisces initiation on the path of the Heart ♓

chapter three

*I go to
prepare
a place
for you...*

*...that where I AM
there
ye may be
also.*

To the Fearless Who Stand Ready
   to Challenge the Last Enemy,

   There comes a time in the life
of every initiate when he must face
the temptation to believe that death
is real.

   In the words of Paul, "The last
enemy that shall be destroyed is
death."[1] And you have read the
words of Serapis Bey,[2] his
admonishment to resist death as the
personification of the energy veil
called evil as well as the impersonal
force that would feign to deprive
every man and woman of the
inheritance of immortality—the gift
of God to his creation.

Somehow, somewhere, through habit and indoctrination, mankind have accepted the concept that the laying down of the physical body, the cessation of life and consciousness and heartbeat in the material form, is the definition of death. This definition is neither scriptural nor is it founded in cosmic law.

As we, then, intensify our effort to merge our consciousness with your own, we can do naught but challenge the record, the memory, and the consciousness of death that lurks as the enemy within the camp at subconscious levels of humanity's awareness.

It should be remembered that at the hour of the crucifixion of our Lord, it is recorded not that he died but that he "gave up the ghost."[3] This wording is a more appropriate explanation of what occurs at the hour of transition.

We define transition as that moment when the soul takes its leave of the physical envelope and makes the transition to the habitation of the etheric body, sometimes called the etheric envelope.

This forcefield of electronic energy vibrates at a level of consciousness just below the ascended master octaves of perfection. It is in the etheric plane that the soul (the individual evolving identity) remains between its incarnations, which continue so long as it is required to evolve in time and space in the planes of Mater.

The 'giving up of the ghost' marks the hour when the breath of the Holy Spirit takes its leave of this mortal coil[4]—this physical forcefield provided by God for a certain cycle of opportunity to prove self-mastery in the physical plane and dimension. If this is not death, then what is death?

As Paul said, "It is appointed unto men once to die." What is this death that all must experience once, "and after this the judgment"?[5] And if living be Christ, as the apostle proclaimed, and dying be gain,[6] then why should this death be resisted as the last enemy?

Clearly there is a death which must be welcomed as the edict of the Lord and a death which must be overcome—and this, too, is his edict.

Come now, and let us reason together, saith the Lord.[7]

That which is real, that which is born of God, created in the image and likeness of the flame of Life itself, cannot die. For the laws of disintegration and death do not apply to that perfect creation which God hath made.[8]

Only that which is unreal can die. And in this context we define death as the cessation of being.

Neither God nor his creation—his offspring, the Christ—can die. But the creation of unreality, of darkness and sin, of the Liar and the lie,[9] is doomed to death from the moment of its inception. For the flame of Life abides not in that creation, and therefore it contains not the momentum of self-perpetuation which only the Seed of God can contain.

Paul says, "Know ye not that so many of us as were baptized into Jesus Christ were baptized into his death?"[10]

Baptism is the infiring of the soul, the form, and the consciousness with a greater measure of Christ-awareness. It is a sacred ritual, a sacrament of the true Church Universal and Triumphant. If, then, we are to come forward to be baptized in Jesus Christ, we must know the meaning of being baptized unto his death.

The death of which Paul speaks is the death of the form of Jesus— the manifestation of the Christ. As the Christ in Jesus laid down that form, it was for a high and holy purpose, that purpose being the death of sin on a planetary scale.

Jesus himself was without blemish and without spot[11]—without negative karma, without any residue of sin from any previous incarnation.[12] Therefore, the laying down of his body temple in that supreme sacrifice was for the balancing of a certain momentum of world sin by the action of the light that coalesced in his body temple and made him not only the living, breathing awareness of the Christ but also the very living presence of the Holy Spirit. His temple was the habitation of the Most High God.

When he made himself the
sacrificial lamb[13] and allowed
himself to be crucified, it was that a
greater concentration of cosmic
energies might be reinforced in the
body of the planet and in the
bodies of all who would ever evolve
upon this planetary home.

By the ritual of the crucifixion,
he increased the action of the light
whereby all who would follow him
in the regeneration[14] could obtain
the greater glory of the resurrection
from the dead. And this
resurrection from the dead is from
the dead consciousness of sin, of
separation from God, of existence
outside the orb of Reality.

"Therefore," said Paul, "we are
buried with him by baptism into
death: that like as Christ was raised
up from the dead by the glory of
the Father, even so we also should
walk in newness of Life."[15]

As we merge our consciousness
and being with that of Jesus the
Christ, we put on the garment of
the Lord's consciousness and of his
experience in the planes of Mater.
And by the grace of God, we are
permitted to experience those

initiations which he went through for the sake of our own soul's reunion with the flame of God.

"For if we have been planted together in the likeness of his death, we shall be also in the likeness of his resurrection: knowing this, that our old man is crucified with him, that the body of sin might be destroyed, that henceforth we should not serve sin. For he that is dead is freed from sin."[16]

Now we come to the plane of the enlightenment of the Buddha. Now we see that that which is destroyed in the baptism of the Holy Ghost and the fire is the body of sin.[17]

Is there anything inherently evil in the physical body of man, of woman, that God has fashioned as the temple of the Holy Spirit? Is the flesh of itself wicked, that it must be condemned to death?

Neither the flesh, nor the stone, nor the twig that is bent can be considered as inherently evil. That which is evil is the consciousness which elects by free will to ensoul darkness, to spawn an energy veil that inhibits life, truth, love, freedom, and all that is sacred and whole.

Thus the body of sin that is destroyed is not the flesh form but it is a conglomerate mass of misqualified energy that has been called the dweller on the threshold and the electronic belt and which consists of the machinations and the evil misrepresentations of Life spawned by that which is known as the carnal mind.[18]

"For he that is dead is freed from sin." This teaching of Paul can be understood only in the light of our definition of death as the cessation of all that is unreal—including sin and the sinful consciousness. For we know that the cessation of life in the physical form does not necessarily free the soul from sin.

For it is written of those who pass from this plane to the next, "He that is filthy, let him be filthy still."[19] We know that the freedom from sin does not come until every jot and tittle of the law is fulfilled.[20]

Therefore, the death of which Paul speaks is the death of the sinful consciousness that is consumed by the sacred fire in the hour of the judgment, the hour of the return of all energies of darkness and light, the hour of the reckoning of the balance of those energies that is made for and on behalf of the soul by the Christ Self in conjunction with the Lords of Karma.

Christ is not dead. He is alive forevermore!

As Jesus was the perfect incarnation of that Christ, as his outer consciousness, the man Jesus, merged so completely with the inner consciousness, with the Christ—so the only death that could be ascribed to him in the ritual of the crucifixion was the death of humanity's awareness of sin.

This he took upon himself that we might have a renewed opportunity to claim Life and to disclaim the lies of the wicked who would have us believe that our true identity that is hid with Christ in God could or would succumb to the laws of dissolution and decay.

"Now if we be dead with Christ, we believe that we shall also live with him: knowing that Christ being raised from the dead dieth no more; death hath no more dominion over him."[21]

Here we see the explanation of that statement "It is given to men once to die."

Once sin and the sinful sense have given way to the fires of the resurrection, there is no more death or dying, neither indeed can be. For the identity of the soul is merged with the Christ, and it is sealed in immortality.

"For in that he died, he died unto sin once: but in that he liveth, he liveth unto God. Likewise reckon ye also yourselves to be dead indeed unto sin, but alive unto God through Jesus Christ our Lord."[22]

Take heed, then, O fellow servants of the Most High God dwelling in the planes of Mater, that you do not succumb to the consciousness of the wicked who know that their time is short and who, when they pass from the screen of life and must stand trial at the Court of the Sacred Fire, know that they indeed will pass through the second death,[23] which is the death of the soul.

For these who have wedded their consciousness to carnality for thousands of years and hundreds of incarnations, there is no hope for a life everlasting. To them death is final. And they mourn when one of their members passes from the screen of life, for they know that this truly is the end of opportunity and of an identity that was bestowed in the beginning as an opportunity to expand God's awareness of himself in the planes of Mater.

As Ramakrishna spoke to Sarada Devi from beyond the grave and told her, "Here I am—where did you think I'd gone to? I've only passed from one room into another,"[24] so I say to you in the words of Jesus: "In my Father's house are many mansions: if it were not so, I would have told you. I go to prepare a place for you . . . that where I AM, there ye may be also."[25]

In the kingdoms of our Lord and his Christ, there is infinite opportunity for the expansion of identity and consciousness that is given to those who have proven in time and space that they will elect to do the will of the Father/Mother God.

And as cycle's door remains ajar, so you will find that each door leads to another room, another plane and dimension where life unfolds life and self realizes more of Self as the flaming identity of God's being.

There is no death for the sons and daughters of God but only eternal victories beyond victories!

The death, then, that must be overcome as the last enemy, the death that must be resisted to the finish, is the temptation to surrender the material form and consciousness before the soul has fulfilled its destiny in and through that form and consciousness.

Therefore, do not welcome this death which is transition but tarry ye in Jerusalem until I come.[26] Tarry you in the plane of Mater until the Christ appears in the full effulgence of the glory of the Second Coming— right within your mind and heart and soul!

Do not accept the lie that you must die in order to be free of sin

but affirm rather the death of the
sinful consciousness here and now
and the perpetuation of life in
this octave as a mandate of
Thy kingdom come, Thy will be done
on earth as it is in heaven!

I AM for you and with you the
victory of immortal fires within
every atom and cell of your being,

Lanello

Christ
the Eternal Link
to Hierarchy

Mediation/Incarnation

for your Aries initiation on the path of the Heart ♈

chapter four

*Christ the Light
which lighteth
<u>every</u> man
that cometh
into the world...*

*...Seeking
to know Him
to love Him
and to be known
and loved of Him.*

My Beloved in Christ,

May I extol to you the virtues of seeking to know Him, to love Him, and to be known and loved of Him.

The Christ is the Mediator— alternating the currents of Spirit and the currents of Mater, weaving the dimensions of God's consciousness as fiery threads of Christic light form the deathless solar body of every soul whom God hath made.

The eternal link to hierarchy is this Christ, this Second Person of the Trinity, that focuses the androgynous nature of God and the potential of God-being for every man, every woman, every child.

"Draw nigh to me, and I will draw nigh to you"[1] is the eternal promise of the I AM Presence.[2]

The Christ is the only means whereby man and woman can draw nigh to the Father/Mother God, whereby the soul can put on the garment of the Lord and merge the spirals of identity until the mortal coil is replaced by the immortal coil in the alchemical fires of truth ever shining, ever available in the very center of Selfhood.

Now I would approach those the world around who are also of this fold,[3] who must also come to the feet of our Lord, and who need the shepherding of their own hallowed Christ Self.

Let not the term "Christ" be a stumbling block to your evolution. Understand that this word has been misused in its application to only one son of God when it should have been the acknowledged birthright of every son and daughter in all ages. For did not this Christ declare through Jesus, "Before Abraham was, I AM"?[4]

Once and for all, let us

establish to Jew and Gentile, Arab and African, Asian and Caucasian that the Christ is the Light which lighteth *every* man that cometh into the world[5]—that the Christ is the potential whereby the soul dwelling in the planes of Mater might realize eternal Godhood in the planes of Spirit.

Those who shun the Christ because they cannot swallow the doctrine and the dogma of a false theology which proclaims only one son as having the opportunity to realize the Christ consciousness must cease from this resistance to truth.

To reject the Messiah in Jesus is to reject the potential for everlasting life within oneself and one's offspring. Those who deny the Christ in Jesus cut off the lifeline of God in themselves. For to deny the Christ Self of any man or woman is to deny that flaming potential within the crucible of one's being.

And therefore, to deny that Christ is certain death. For no individuality can have the permanence of Reality outside the consciousness of the Christ.

This is the law of the polarity of the cosmos, of the spirals of Alpha and Omega, and of the cross that depicts the merging of Spirit and Mater at the nexus, which represents the awareness of being as the Christ in self and in all.

This is why that statement is made that "at the name of Jesus every knee should bow, of things in heaven, and things in earth, and things under the earth; and that every tongue should confess that Jesus Christ is Lord, to the glory of God the Father."[6]

In every age, the Lord God has sent forth his representatives to show forth the effulgence of the Logos in Christed beings—"male and female created he them."[7] If those among mankind for whom the example is given fail to acknowledge that Christ as the Mediator in the avatar that is sent, then their own opportunity for the realization of the Christ is cut off.

This is the law, and it cannot be broken.

Therefore, it is not the man or the outer person that we worship, for this would be idolatry. But to fail to acknowledge the Christ incarnate as the avatar of the age—this is indeed blasphemy and the sin against the Holy Spirit which cannot be forgiven until it is forsaken.[8]

In this hour at the conclusion of the twentieth century, all mankind are given the opportunity to return to the feet of the Godhead through that blessed Mediator, the Holy Christ Self.

If you will begin to acknowledge the Christ in those who have set forth the example in this age and in all past ages—in Abraham and Isaac, in Elijah and Elisha, in Enos and Enoch, in the prophets and kings of Israel, in yourself and in the members of your family—you will soon come to know, by the activation of the energies of that veritable divine flow, that Christ lived also in Jesus, in Mary, in Joseph, and in the emissaries of the Great White Brotherhood[9] who have appeared down through the centuries in every race, in every nation.

Therefore let none deny, let all

confess that the Christ is Lord, is priest and prophet, king and queen who reigns supreme in every incarnation of God!

It is not necessary to bind yourselves to any religious creed, to any organization, in order to have the blessing and the proximity of the Christ mind. Here and now, you who read my words can be converted through the true doctrine and the tenets of the Great White Brotherhood that are the foundation of the Church Universal and Triumphant.[10]

This church shall be the ultimate manifestation of the light of the City Foursquare[11] upon this planet in this age and in all ages to come. And you who read my words and understand this concept for the first time, who would come into the fold of hierarchy, consider yourselves a part of the body of God and a part of the true church when, by your acceptance of the Christ, you can acknowledge that Light both in Jesus and in yourself.

The Darjeeling Council desires to see a great swelling of the people of Terra, a merging of hearts afire

with this cosmic conception of souls
who, having found their identity in
God, are ready to take the ultimate
stand in defense of the freedom of
every man, woman, and child to
likewise pursue and find that same
identity in Christ.

We who desire to intensify
Reality within you can do so only
through the Christ flame within the
heart—only through that Mediator
whose being manifests at once in
heaven and on earth.

Paul understood how the Christ
is that essential element of being
that translates the things in heaven,
the things in earth, and the things
under the earth. The Christ is the
aspect of us all that simultaneously
occupies all dimensions of God's
being in Father and in Mother, in
Spirit and in Matter.

It is through Christ that I speak
to you. My beloved on earth
receives the impartations of my
mind. In the merging, then, of our
being, we are one in Christ, who is
the fulcrum of our oneness. Let,
then, that Christ be in you and
claim thereby your oneness with
hierarchy, your twin flame, your

counterpart in heaven, and all of the evolutions of God on this and other worlds.

Do you not see, O precious hearts, how the fallen ones have attempted to deprive you of oneness by denying the coming of the Messiah and by promising always a future hope, a future glory, and a future resurrection?

But all these things can be yours here and now through the determined acceptance of the Light of being that is within you now—for whom you need not wait. For he has been waiting a long while to be received in your soul, in your heart, and in your mind.

Let the bells ring out! Let the joybells of the temples at etheric planes ring now the true message of salvation—that all mankind can be free in the resurrection and the resurgence of the realities of being!

And let all that has opposed the Christ as antichrist,[12] as the carnal mind, and as the complications of the fallen ones[13] be exposed as the deception of those who are unreal and whose claim to Reality is supported only by the credulity of the blind leaders and their followers.[14]

I stand upon Mount Horeb and I proclaim the Word of Moses: "I AM the Lord thy God, which have brought thee out of the land of Egypt, out of the house of bondage."[15] I proclaim the deliverance of the Israelites from the age-old deceptions of the carnal mind, of the Liar and his lie.

By the name of the Lord I AM THAT I AM, which was revealed to Moses,[16] I say, be free this day!

Yours for the victory of the Mediator,

Lanello

The LAW of CYCLES

The Rhythmic Equation of God in Man

*O*ne of the great sources of comfort that has come to me in this life has been an understanding and a perception of the mathematical law and formula of the Law of Cycles whereby Spirit cycles through Matter and Matter cycles through Spirit.

We approach the Law of Cycles with reverence for the Creator whose Self-expression it contains. All evidence of its outworking in man, the earth, the elements, and the stars are but the tracings of his Being, footprints in the sands, tracks in the upper snows. Wherever we behold his markings as cyclings of infinity tumbling through the finite coils of time and space, there he has been. There his awful, wonderful Presence is—just beyond the veiled spirals of his creation.

Attempting to penetrate the Law of Cycles, we find secrets sublime and all-encompassing— the being of man the microcosm, in man the Macrocosm. These secrets have remained closely guarded by the adepts of the mystery schools for thousands of years, for an understanding of these laws provides a predictable platform of evolution—and the power to initiate cycles of our own.

Kuthumi's Work on Cycles

The Ascended Master Kuthumi has influenced science and world thought for thousands of years. And it is he who has taught the Law of Cycles as fundamental to a comprehensive world view.

Embodied as the great master Pythagoras, Kuthumi expounded the law of the harmony of opposing forces. He taught how all of manifestation is composed of vibration in various states of interaction and equilibrium. We will see how this profound understanding is inherent in the cyclic law.

During the 1800s, Kuthumi—known to his Western students as Koot Hoomi Lal Singh, or K.H.—was an advanced adept. He had conquered the usual ravages of time on the physical form, and it is said that for decades he continued to have the same youthful appearance. He was able to control the elements and to project a double of his physical body anywhere on the planet to perform his duties or to teach his disciples.

Much of his life remains a mystery, but we know he directed the course of the Theosophical Society from an esoteric school of adepts in a remote Himalayan valley inaccessible to anyone uninvited. Below him were advanced chelas (students). Above him were several Chohans (Lords, or Masters) and the Maha Chohan. The strictest codes of esoteric discipline were kept.

Kuthumi taught with profound scholarship, and he had a mind able to penetrate the veils of time and read the *akashic* records of earth's history. The knowledge of his Chohans was of intergalactic dimensions, and they guided him closely in all of his dealings with his chelas. Much to the wonder of his fellow adepts and to the consternation of his Chohans, Kuthumi attempted to bring to Western man some of the long forbidden mysteries of the occult Brotherhood.

In a letter sent to the English philosopher A. O. Hume in 1882, published in the book *The Mahatma Letters*, Kuthumi wrote, "I would not refuse what I have a right to teach. Only I had to study for fifteen years before I came to the doctrines of cycles and had to learn simpler things at first."

Think of it! The Master we have come to know and love

The galaxy
is spinning out
its spiral arms in space.
The cosmic magnet
drives the heart of worlds
—fluids of Life pulsating
in a rhythmic ebb and flow.
Chromosomes align in precise array.
Behold the miracle of creation.
Gaze into the deep night sky
and see the pulsar beating in perfect time.
Drink the words of the poet as he sings in perfect rhyme.
The electron in cyclic rhythm with the proton.
The planets in rhythm with the sun.
The solar system in rhythm with the galaxy.
Reverberations of the spheres in space
echo in the silence of our meditation.
There is harmony in God's creation!
There is rhythm. There is flow.
And cycles turn the wheels of time
as the Great Mother
nurtures the procession of Life.

Elizabeth Clare Prophet

as friend on the Path had to study fifteen years under the Chohans before coming to the subject of the Law of Cycles. It is by dispensation of the Lords of Mind that we today shall penetrate some of these teachings, along with the revelations brought forth by the Ascended Masters.

Where shall we start our excursion through the vast ocean of God's creation? The wonder of it all is that no matter where we start, by following any cycle of Life to its origin, there we stand gazing face-to-face with God. For he is the originator of all cycles. He is the driving force spinning at the pivot point of all form.

The Cycle Defined

A cycle is an interval of time during which a sequence of a recurring succession of events or phenomena is completed. It is also defined as a "recurrent sequence of events which occur in such order that the last event of one sequence immediately precedes the recurrence of the first event in a new series."

Place your hand on your heart and feel the cycles of your heart's pulsation, the beat of your physical life sustaining the vehicles of your soul's evolution in Matter. Look up at a light bulb and know that it shines because electricity is pulsating at a cycle of sixty times per second through its filament. Listen to a piece of music and hear the cyclic vibration of the violin strings resonating through the eardrum as sound.

All of Cosmos can be comprehended in terms of cycles. The warp and woof of creation is manifest in currents of spiritual sound vibrating according to cyclic law. The very

Pythagoras delivered the mathematical truths of the law of cycles to his spiritual community at Crotona, Italy in the sixth century B.C. All of Cosmos, he taught, is comprehensible through numbers because the material universe is born from their very essence. By knowing the secret of the numbers behind cosmic cycles, the initiate could approach a powerful understanding of the workings of the universe. So vast were the implications of this knowledge that the Pythagoreans kept it in strictest silence, sharing it with no uninitiated man. This great master understood how music expressed the harmonic ratios of mathematics and used "musical medicine" to heal both body and soul.

atoms and electrons of this world of form bow to the cyclic interchange of Spirit into Matter, Matter into Spirit—all-encompassed in the one element from which all of Life issues forth.

The marriage of science and true religion brings forth the progeny of wisdom and higher understanding. Some of the elements of the Law of Cycles we will discuss clash with what is regarded as current scientific fact or archaeological proofs.

In the same letter of 1882 to Hume, in explaining how exact a science the esoteric teachings were, Kuthumi wrote, "Let me tell you that the means we avail ourselves of are all laid down for us in a code as old as humanity to the minutest detail, but every one of us has to begin from the beginning, not from the end. Our laws are as immutable as those of Nature, and they were known to man and eternity before this strutting gamecock, modern science, was hatched."

A hundred years have passed since that letter, and indeed the cycle has turned. Science is beginning to prove with her instruments and detectors many laws and facts previously considered to be occult meanderings.

The Cosmic Magnet

To understand one of the basic tenets of the Law of Cycles, we must delve into the deepest mysteries of our Spirit/Matter universe. Here we contact the simplest and grandest of all cycles: the dual pulsation that is the heartbeat of Cosmos. Here we find the one element, forever in equilibrium, forever

CYCLES OF COSMO

*C*ycles of man, Nature, and Cosmos often interact in the most remarkable and intricate ways. We see here graphic examples of the Hermetic axiom, "As Above, so below," showing how the microcosmic cycles of man reflect the macrocosmic cycles of God, and how the processes of Nature move with cyclic precision.

Writing to a disciple in *The Mahatma Letters*, the great Master K.H. (Kuthumi) wrote:

As you may infer by analogy every globe [planet] before it reaches its adult period, has to pass through a formation period—also septenary [seven-fold]. Law in nature is uniform and the conception, formation, birth, progress and development of the child differs from those of the globe only in magnitude.

The globe has two periods of teething and capillature—its first rocks which it also sheds to make room for new—and its ferns and mosses before it gets forest. As the atoms in the body change [every] seven years, so does the globe renew its strata every seven cycles... The correspondence between a mother-globe and her child-man may be thus worked out. Both have their seven principles.

In Hindu philosophy there are four cyclic ages called yugas that follow one after another in the physical and spiritual evolution of man. It is said that the duration of our present Kali Yuga is 432,000 years. The combined duration of all four ages, each with a specific length, is 4,320,000. In one hour, our hearts beat 4,320 times, mirroring the 4-3-2 number which recurs in many other cycles as well.

The precession of the equinoxes is the time it takes the sun to make a complete circuit along the backdrop of the zodiacal constellations. This cycle takes 25,920 years to complete. In twenty-four hours, we breathe 25,920 times. The celestial cycle has its counterpart in the body of man.

Studies of the 11.1-year cycle of sunspots report that they are directly related to magnetic conditions here on earth and correspond to peaks in the incidence of epidemics and social, economic, and political unrest.

Earthquakes also follow a cycle about eleven years long. The greatest number of quakes occur about the same time as most sunspots. Also, irregularities in the earthquake cycle seem to correspond to irregularities in the sunspot cycle.

Japanese Dr. Maki Takata found that the composition of human blood changes in relation to the 11-year sunspot cycle, to solar flares, and during eclipses.

Changes in the earth's crust seem to correspond to the moon's position. It has been estimated that the city of Moscow rises and falls nearly twenty inches, twice a day, in response to the moon's gravitational pull.

Oysters rhythmically open their shells widest twice a day at high tide when the moon is exerting its maximum gravitational effect on the earth. One scientist removed oysters from New Haven, Connecticut to an Evanston, Illinois laboratory and noted that in about two weeks they had reset their motions to the Evanston lunar phases—opening their shells widest at the precise time when there would have been a high tide in Evanston if there had been an ocean. The oysters responded to the moon's force even though they were kept in a darkened room.

The grunion, a small fish of Southern California, spawn only when the tidal cycle is most favorable for the survival of its young. Every two weeks, from March to August, the grunion wiggle up onto the beach to lay and fertilize eggs on the night following the highest tide. In this way their eggs are undisturbed until the next high tide two weeks later when the egg membranes burst under the force of the waves to release the matured fish.

When researchers placed pieces of potato with sprouting eyes in a hermetically-sealed container in complete darkness and under constant pressure, they found that the potato had a 24-hour cycle of oxygen consumption directly related to the 24-hour cycle of barometric pressure outside the container. Most surprising was the potato's ability to accurately predict the outside barometric pressure two days in advance. With further experimentation, the researchers found that every living thing they studied—from carrots to seaweed, and from crabs and oysters to rats—could predict barometric pressure changes two days in advance.

Seemingly unrelated phenomena occur every 9.2 years. This interval marks cycles in grasshopper population, Lake Michigan water level, alternate thickness of tree rings, business failures, pig iron and copper prices, industrial stock prices, and railroad stock prices.

pulsating in the rhythmic cycles that reverberate down to the inner core of every atom.

The entire religious philosophy of the yin/yang of Taoism is built upon the existence and importance of the cyclic interchange between an infinite hierarchy of opposing, or complementary, forces. It is the grand cycle of Alpha-to-Omega.

We hear it singing the song of the atom within our very own cosmos. It is the inhalation and exhalation of the Godhead. It is the interdimensional pattern of flow between Spirit and Matter—in Sanskrit, *Puruśa* and *Prakṛti*—the two poles of the cosmic magnet that sustains all of Life. Truly, our study of the Law of Cycles is a meditation on our own inner Being.

We read in *Climb the Highest Mountain*, "The Truth all mankind seek is based on the irrefutable law that Spirit and Matter are not opposites: they are the twofold nature of God's Being which remain forever as the Divine Polarity."

This primary cycle we are considering is the simplest relationship of two forces—and the most all-encompassing action. If we clearly embrace the cyclic flow and unity between the Spirit/Matter, or Father/Mother principles of motion, it is as if we are given a library card to God's storehouse of universal knowledge.

As Kuthumi said, let us begin at the beginning, and all of the vast complexities of God's infinite cycles will become clear upon the illuminated background of the original cycle.

All form is the result of motion. To have motion implies a point toward which the motion occurs and away from which it proceeds. This, in its grandest conception, is the cosmic magnet, the Father/Mother flow.

A magnet attracts and a magnet repels. If you hold a horseshoe magnet in your hand, you can discover that there is a point of perfect equilibrium in the space exactly between the two opposite poles. At the heart of the polarity is unity and harmony.

All of Cosmos is a magnet in the Macrocosmic sense. In his Pearl of Wisdom of June 1968, Sanat Kumara—known throughout religious literary history as "the Ancient of Days"—teaches about this cycle of universal flow:

"Those who would explore the far reaches of space, both inner and outer, should understand that the Divine Feminine is the womb of creation which is impregnated with Life by the

Spirit of God. The material universe is the negative polarity whereas the spiritual universe is the positive polarity of the Godhead. Matter, meaning *Mater* [Latin for Mother], is the chalice that receives the invigorating, Life-giving essence of the sacred fire. Thus the Father principle completes the cycle of manifestation in the world of form through the Mother aspect, and child-man is nourished by the balancing, sustaining action of Life whose twofold nature [Spirit/Matter, masculine/feminine] is epitomized in the Christ."

This divine polarity exists throughout Cosmos—from the balanced pulsation of the Great Central Sun to the systemic equilibrium of the hydrogen atom.

We learn from the science of sound and from the archives of the Brotherhood that all manifested Cosmos is the interplay of vibrations—a vast web of electromagnetic waves oscillating at different numbers of cycles per second. And what is a vibration if not a cyclic motion related to a framework of time and space orientation?

The range of cycles is infinite—from one cycle in billions of years to billions of cycles each second. All are derivatives of the one pulsation we observe pivoting around the point of infinite equilibrium of the cosmic magnet.

The Grand Cycle

Before we become immersed in this web of creation, let us take a step up our mountain of observation and consider the grandest, longest, most mysterious cycle in the world of

---

We see a chain of cycles placed on a grid of the golden ratio. Let us imagine that we are floating above this expanding spiral, looking down into its receding central cycle—which disappears into the infinite past. Each cycle of evolution takes in more of God. Each round sends us into wider spheres of the body of God's Cosmos. Each new emergence from the period of *pralaya* brings us forth into a new, higher creation, ever spiraling upwards from glory unto glory— into the endless realms of infinity. With perfect mathematical precision, these cycles follow the vast spiral of transcendence based upon the golden ratio.

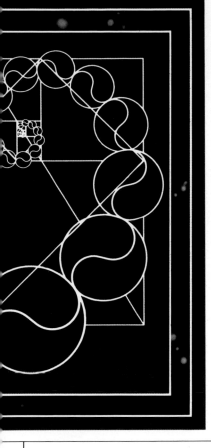

form. The length of this cycle is calculated in terms of trillions of years, and we find ourselves reaching for a volume that might be called the Life of Brahma.

Writing from the home of Kuthumi at Tzigadze in the Himalayas, gazing at an iceberg before him, Morya, one of the adepts who guided the Theosophical Society, wrote to A. P. Sinnett in January of 1882: "Nothing in nature springs into existence suddenly, all being subjected to the same law of gradual evolution. Realize but once the process of the maha cycle, of one sphere, and you have realized them all. One man is born like another man, one race evolves, develops, and declines like another and all other races. Nature follows the same groove from the 'creation' of a universe down to that of a mosquito. In studying esoteric cosmogony keep a spiritual eye upon the physiological process of human birth; proceed from cause to effect. . . . Cosmology is the physiology of the universe spiritualized, for there is but one law."

We will do just that. First we will learn of the cycles of Brahma, of God, as he unfolds the myriad systems of worlds. Then we will learn of man the microcosm. Eventually, the cycles of becoming will spread before us.

Man has always pondered the mysteries of creation. Scientists through the ages—astronomers, cosmologists, physicists—have developed various scenarios of the beginning of the universe.

The steady state theory postulates no beginning or ending—just a steady eternal state of nontranscendence.

The big bang theory states that around fifteen billion years ago all of matter we know of was compressed into an infinitely small ball of cosmic dust. All of a sudden, the big bang—and the physical universe was born. The explosion occurred and life began to evolve from the atomic subparticle to our present universe.

Those who believe in this theory quietly hide their eyes from the question, "What came before the big bang? What was the cause behind the effect?"

Though the theory may explain one aspect of one cycle of cosmic evolution, it doesn't provide the framework for an integrated and all-embracing cosmo-conception.

Let us reach for the deeper perspective held

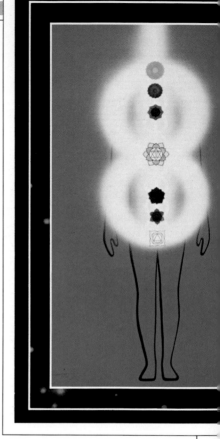

in the retreats of the Brotherhood in the heart of the Himalayas. Not material scientists but great scientists of the Spirit, the Ascended Masters and cosmic beings can provide infant mankind with a perspective that spans endless eternities of creation.

In their view, the Law of Cycles is the key to the alternating cycles of the explosion and implosion of the Matter universes as they proceed in and out of Spirit.

Exploring the *Purāṇas*

From the ancient epochs of India, history has preserved a series of writings called the *Purāṇas*. These are the teachings of great masters originally recorded in an extremely remote period in earth's history.

Scientists and spiritual healers have proven that the body of man is a magnet. All magnets create cycles of positive and negative flow, yet there is always a point of perfect equilibrium between the two polarities. As prana flows through our system, the heart is the point of balance. But the point of perfect harmony is beyond the physical heart—in the secret chamber of the heart. It is from this point of peace and power that we can send forth the auric emanations to heal not only our personal microcosm but also the world outside the boundary of our skin.

The word *Purāṇa* means "that which lives from ancient times," or "the records of ancient events." There are generally five subjects covered in these most ancient writings: 1) the creation of the universe; 2) re-creation after destruction or deluge; 3) the genealogy of the gods and teachers; 4) the *manvantaras*, or *Manu-antaras*, the great periods of time with the *Manu* as the primal ancestor; and, finally, 5) the histories of the Solar and Lunar dynasties.

One of the great *Purāṇas* is called the *Bhagavata Purāṇa*. In section III, the revered teacher Maitreya sets forth the revelation of the cycles of cosmic creation. He teaches about the days and nights of Brahma and the infinite cycles of beginnings and endings and new beginnings. We now shake the dust from this ancient text, totally neglected by Western historians, as we read these ancient records from Lord Maitreya to his pupil Vidura.

"O Vidura, beyond the three worlds...a day consists of one thousand cycles of four yugas. The night is also of the same duration when the creator of the universe goes to sleep. At the end of the night, the creation of the world starts and proceeds so long as it is God Brahma's day which covers the period of fourteen Manus."

In the chronology of the Hindus, one day of Brahma is said to be four billion, three hundred and twenty million years.

Continuing Maitreya's discourse to his pupil Vidura: "Every Manu rules during his own period which is somewhat longer than seventy-one cycles [each consisting] of four yugas."

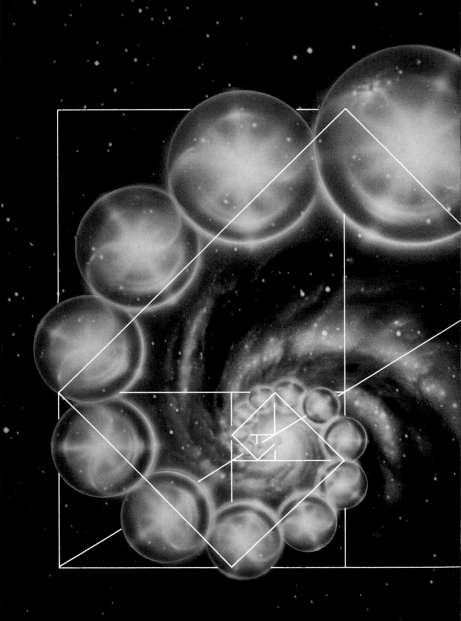

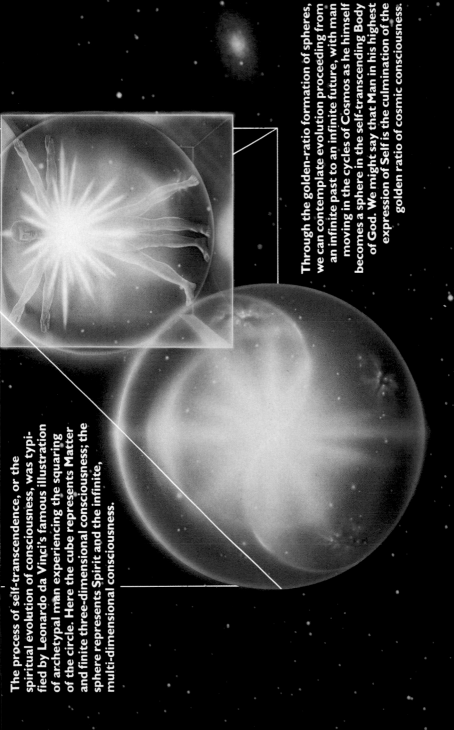

The process of self-transcendence, or the spiritual evolution of consciousness, was typified by Leonardo da Vinci's famous illustration of archetypal man experiencing the squaring of the circle. Here the cube represents Matter and finite three-dimensional consciousness; the sphere represents Spirit and the infinite, multi-dimensional consciousness.

Through the golden-ratio formation of spheres, we can contemplate evolution proceeding from an infinite past to an infinite future, with man moving in the cycles of Cosmos as he himself becomes a sphere in the self-transcending Body of God. We might say that Man in his highest expression of Self is the culmination of the golden ratio of cosmic consciousness.

Yuga is the Sanskrit word for a "world-period." The Sanskrit names for the four *yugas* are *Satya Yuga, Tretā Yuga, Dvāpara Yuga,* and *Kali Yuga.* Each successive age brings with it a different stage of civilization and a different mode of man's consciousness. In each of the *yugas,* man is given the spiritual tools that most effectively assist him to succeed in the cycles of evolution.

Just as the Great Cycle of Brahma's life is the archetype of man's personal cycles, so it is true with the *yugas.* The four *yugas* span millions of years in spheres of cosmic evolution, but we are taught that man himself goes through innumerable cycles of his own four *yugas*—as he walks the rounds toward reunion with God. We can compare the cycles of the evolution of the soul in the mastery of the four lower bodies, the four quadrants of being, with the cyclings of the four *yugas.* Thus the mastery of time and space is built upon this Law of Cycles.

One hundred cosmic years constitutes the life of Brahma. This is regarded as a whole period of Brahma's age, called the *Mahā Kalpa,* or "Great Cycle." It is the longest single cycle we can detect. We are told that its duration is three hundred eleven trillion, forty billion years in length.

Maitreya continues in the *Bhagavata Purāṇa,* "Half of the life [of God Brahma] is called parārdha. The first parārdha [of his life] has passed. Now the other half is running." In our great cycle, our *Mahā Kalpa,* we have turned past the axial point of the course of Cosmos.

God has once again exhaled his breath of Life as fohat and the long inbreath has begun to return all to the spiritual source once again. The beginningless, endless cycle—as all things emanate from and return to the One.

God has neither beginning nor ending because his being takes in the universe of cycles and all that precedes and follows them in the formed and unformed dimensions of Spirit. But for a brief interim man seems to have a beginning and an ending because he identifies with a slice of the spiral that initiates in Spirit, evolves through Matter, and returns to Spirit.

When outer man becomes congruent with the spiritual essence of his own Divine Monad, he then becomes the drop merging into the ocean of God. Our individualized personalities had a beginning in the warp and woof of manifestation, but the core of the atom of our being, our spiritual Monad, began when God himself began.

The Law of Karma

The Law of Karma, of perfect retribution, is intimately related to the Law of Cycles.

We can know with absolute surety that if we send out hatred or negative vibrations, sooner or later they will cycle back to ourselves—and we will have to expend energy to revibrate our murky creation.

We can also know that the self-generated impulse toward God, toward good, toward service of our fellowman will, with infinite precision, cycle back also and add to our momentum of light and our return to wholeness. This is the Law of Karma. It is the mathematically predictable Law of Cycles. It is the most simple yet profound manifestation of justice.

By willingly coming into congruence with the cycle of involution, evolution, and ascension, we know that at the end of this round we will indeed see the face of God.

Can we imagine what it would be like if the Law of Cycles didn't exist, if we had no way of knowing where to direct our striving to return to a state of wholeness?

To recapitulate what we have learned, there is the endless rhythmic pulsation of cosmic creation called in the East the *Mahā Kalpa,* or Great Cycle. Though there are infinite cycles within cycles, the overall flow consists of an outbreath and an inbreath, an Alpha thrust of creation followed by the Omega return to the heart of Brahma. At the end of each creative cycle is the *pralaya,* which is the Sanskrit word for the "period of rest." At best, then, the big bang theory becomes a crude statement of the sublime cosmic moment of the birth of worlds when the sine wave passes from imperceptible to perceptible reality—that is, from what we call Spirit to what we call Matter.

Delving deeper into the mysteries of creation, we come to the awareness that all is Spirit. All forms of Matter—even the densest physical substance—are the crystallized fire mist of spiritual essence. The successive lives of Brahma can be conceived of by our limited minds as immense cyclic arcs of pure Spirit involuting into the veils of denser Matter,

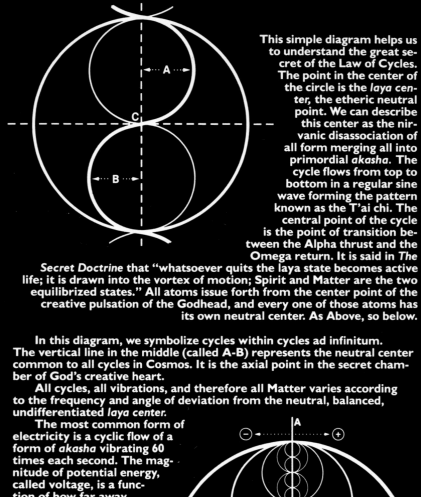

This simple diagram helps us to understand the great secret of the Law of Cycles. The point in the center of the circle is the *laya center*, the etheric neutral point. We can describe this center as the nirvanic disassociation of all form merging all into primordial *akasha*. The cycle flows from top to bottom in a regular sine wave forming the pattern known as the T'ai chi. The central point of the cycle is the point of transition between the Alpha thrust and the Omega return. It is said in *The Secret Doctrine* that "whatsoever quits the laya state becomes active life; it is drawn into the vortex of motion; Spirit and Matter are the two equilibrized states." All atoms issue forth from the center point of the creative pulsation of the Godhead, and every one of those atoms has its own neutral center. As Above, so below.

In this diagram, we symbolize cycles within cycles ad infinitum. The vertical line in the middle (called A-B) represents the neutral center common to all cycles in Cosmos. It is the axial point in the secret chamber of God's creative heart.

All cycles, all vibrations, and therefore all Matter varies according to the frequency and angle of deviation from the neutral, balanced, undifferentiated *laya center*.

The most common form of electricity is a cyclic flow of a form of *akasha* vibrating 60 times each second. The magnitude of potential energy, called voltage, is a function of how far away from the neutral center of the cycle the energy has been made to flow. The greater the distance, the more energy available because there is a greater polarity built between the plus and minus crests of the cycle. The same is true in the world of man and Spirit. Man can send out greater or lesser vibrations of energy from the power center in his heart.

and then evolving back to the ethereal, spiritual origin.

Our relative position in the grand cycle of our personal or planetary cycle can be understood as the ratio of Spirit to Matter. As Brahma outbreathes the web of creation, there is a densification as the universe puts on its seven coats of skins.

An axial point is reached in the cycle where the outbreath is expended and inbreath begins. It is the point of the lowest descent of the arc of Spirit into Matter. It is the state of equilibrium of the positive and negative poles of the cosmic magnet. It is the halfway point in the cycle that Maitreya mentioned we have passed.

Then there is the period of return to Spirit. All that has become involved in material form begins its process of etherealization and return to the one Source—and to the period of *pralayic* rest—once again to begin a new cycle of becoming.

The Law of Transcendence

As we ponder the immense odyssey of God's being through eternal rounds of beginnings and endings, we can ask the fateful question: Why? What is the purpose of it all if the universe is just an endless cycle of rounds with man floating on a speck of dust in space cast loose on a shoreless ocean? What is the nature of the Godhead as he exists through endless cycles in infinite space?

The answer, we are told, is that the Law of Cycles implements the Law of Transcendence. God is a transcendent being, and with each new outbreath he evolves to a greater state of cosmic perfection and beauty.

The cycles are not really circles or sine waves but they are spirals—spirals of infinite expansion according to the geometry of the golden ratio (1:1.618. . .). Each cycle of evolution takes in more of God. Each round sends us into wider spheres of the body of God's Cosmos.

The individualities enmeshed in the fabric of the Godhead eventually reach a point in evolution where they span the cyclic lifetimes of Brahma. With each new pulsation, after each successive *pralaya*, the imprint of higher planes of perfection impregnate the gestating cosmic egg.

The endless cyclic patterns of cosmic evolution would be an abominable injustice if not for the fact that each new cycle begins at a higher point of perfection. This universe is not an infernal merry-go-round that spins in space.

What meaningless boredom, what hellish drudgery it would be to have to return forever to the same place in the cycle like a broken record. God and all of his creation is continually transcending itself, with the leading edge of consciousness always able to contact new vistas of infinity and to create greater manifestations of divine purpose.

How does man the individual fit into this vast cosmic plan of transcendent cycles? How can we apply the Law of Cycles for the purpose of greater acceleration around the rings of initiation?

The Law of Correspondence

In the far-distant past, Hermes, Messenger of the Gods, delivered to us the nucleus of the Law of Cycles—"As Above, so below."

We still retain what is called the "Emerald Tablet" of Hermes. This short but concise teaching formed the core of the most ancient masonic orders and schools of the Brotherhood. It begins with these words:

> True, without any error;
> certain, very true;
> That which is Above,
> is as that which is below;
> and that which is below,
> is as That which is Above;
> For achieving the wonders of the Universe.

This is the Law of Analogy, the Law of Correspondence, and it provides us with the sense of divine order which is indeed the sense of justice.

The Law of Correspondence states that the creation corresponds to the Creator, that man corresponds to God. Therefore, the Real Image of man is congruent with his God Source by design, by intent, by law.

The design is one of transcendent cycles, mirrored all the way through the veils of Matter into the coil of the densest atom.

The intent is for man the individual to become a beneficent co-creator with the Godhead, to span cosmic cycles, to be the one who breathes out galactic systems and provides the impulse of coherent love that binds the particulate atoms into a meaningful platform of evolution.

The law is the law of recurrent cycles ever transcending the previous round. The Law of Transcendence offers us the comfort of the highest hope.

As the cycles of Cosmos spiral upward into greater and greater dimensions, so man can forever transcend the veils of Matter that form the schoolrooms for his soul's evolution. The transcendent teaching of the Christ reveals infinite possibilities for God and man. It destroys the lie of eternal damnation. It opens the door of opportunity for repentance and healing. It is absolute justice in manifestation.

"Man—the oversoul and God to a vast universe of his inner identity"

It is not easy for mortal man to stretch his mind beyond the boundaries of infinity. Maitreya has taught that a lifetime of Brahma, a universe lasting trillions of years, appears as a single atom when merged in the body of the great *Puruśa*. The planets spinning around our sun are like one atom in the body of the Milky Way galaxy—the galaxy having over a hundred billion sun centers, each with its own system of worlds. The being ensouling the galaxy is aware of our world as an atom in his body, teeming with sentient life evolving.

And then there is man—the oversoul and God to a vast universe of his inner identity. We are cells in the Body of God, and we have fifty trillion cells that compose our body. Each one of those cells has intelligence, has a spark of divinity. Think of it. Each one of our cells considers us as the Godhead of its universe, the originator of its life impulses. Paul said, "Know ye not that ye are the temple of God, and that the Spirit of God dwelleth in you?"

How far along the vibratory spectrum of cosmic life can we go in each direction?

Who is to say that there isn't a complex system of life-forms resident on the surface of each electron as it spins in polar equilibrium to its nuclear sun center—just as our earthy sphere of cosmic dust spins around its sun, teeming with life? The mortal mind cannot tell. But beings with vast awareness have told us that the cycles of God are infinite in all directions.

Let us consider man the microcosm, who is also the Macrocosm, and behold the workings of cyclic law as we trace the course of man's evolution in the hierarchical ladder of being.

Let us first consider man and his indivisible parts and define thereby which portion of man travels along the endless cycles of evolution.

Man—the Microcosm

Man is a sevenfold creation. The Great White Brotherhood has always taught that the number seven is the primary harmonic quantity. Man is composed of seven sheaths, or bodies, bestowed upon him by the Lords of Form who, in turn, are sevenfold in their own nature.

Pythagoras explained the theory of the eternal Monad to his inner disciples. According to the adept Kuthumi, the reincarnation of Master Pythagoras, the Monad can be considered as the upper two principles of man's sevenfold being.

It is this reflective spark of divinity that sends forth our soul to cycle through the veils of maya. And through the threefold flame this soul constructs around itself the temporary lower vehicles used to draw in experience of God's nature. It is the sacred fire infolding more and more of itself.

"The riddle of eternity and evolution is contained within the symbol of the circle— a cross section of a spiral."

The Divine Monad exists even after the transition called death, while the lower bodies dissipate according to the cyclic laws of their substance. All of substance in Matter is subject to the Law of Cycles governing integration and disintegration, or the manifestation of form and the return to formlessness.

The soul is the as-yet-nonpermanent atom in God's Body. It is infused with the germinal seed to become ruler of a cosmos. This it must do by the exercise of free will.

It is the soul as the extension of the I AM Presence and causal body that is given opportunity to spin the 'Deathless Solar Body' out of the fibers of *akasha*.

The Circle of Life

The riddle of eternity and evolution is contained within the symbol of the circle—a cross section of a spiral that has neither beginning nor ending but appears to be finite as it passes through the physical universe in the form of planets, stars, galaxies, and man himself.

The circle is the two-dimensional representation of the spiral cycle that begins in the square base of the pyramid and rises to the apex of realization in the capstone of Life. And there in the center of the capstone, the Law of Transcendence functions through the eye of God. For when the spiral passes through the All-Seeing Eye, it transcends the dimensions of form and passes from Matter to Spirit.

This is the fulfillment of the Law of Cycles that begins in the heart of God and culminates in every perfect creation. Energy that begins as a spiral in Spirit descends into Matter, there to coalesce around the flame and then—in the twinkling of an eye—to return to Spirit over the descending and ascending spirals of God's consciousness. God himself is the circle that has neither beginning nor ending of cycles, though we can detect the pulsations of his inbreath and outbreath.

The heavenly bodies are undergoing cyclic evolution within the larger infinite spiral of God's being in Spirit—passing through material manifestation and returning to Spirit. In the Macrocosm as well as in the microcosm, circling spirals trigger the flow of energy into and out of form.

Throughout the universe, the pattern of cyclic return is reproduced again and again with infinite precision, traversing realms of eternity, expanding according to the golden ratio.

Man as Co-Creator

Although the circle itself is without beginning or ending, at any point on the circumference of the circle, the hand of God may draw an intersecting line, thereby creating a beginning and an ending. Thus cycles are initiated and worlds are born.

The whirl of *fohatic* release, directed by the guiding

will of a God-free being, can send reverberating vibrations careening through space. Drop a stone into a still pond and watch the cyclic wave patterns continue to flow and flow in smooth rhythm. Drop a stone into an agitated pond, and there results a complex of wave pattern interchange, but the cycle initiated by the stone continues to affect the water. Thus it is by the hand of God and by his emissaries.

Once man has passed through the cycles of the initiatic process—the spirals of destiny that unlock the total pattern of his identity—he earns the right to be congruent with the dot

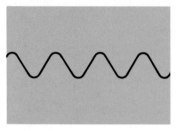

in the center of the great circle of Life. That dot in the center of the circle is the point of dynamic equilibrium resident in all of creation.

There is always that central point of balance, called the *laya center* in Hindu esoteric science. To become one with this power center, this dot of equilibrium in the center of God's circle, is to be able to direct the power of *fohat* as it courses along the vibratory pathways we create.

Visualize a simple sine wave. This represents a rhythmic cycle of a particular frequency. There is a rising curve, then a falling curve, and then a rising curve, and so forth. According to the Law of Cycles, there must be a force that pulls the current of God's undifferentiated energy into the rising curve. And there must be an opposite force that attracts this stream of energy (represented by the line) into the falling curve. These are the positive and negative poles active at the core of all cycles.

To be the dot in the center of the circle is to become the harmony of the polar forces—to be the axis in the spinning sphere of creative force. It is the pivot point of cyclic flow. It is reached in samadhi. It is utilized by adepts to control the fire of space.

All of manifested Cosmos is the interplay of cyclic vibrations, initiated somewhere, somehow, by someone. As we ascend the scales of evolution, we are entrusted with the divine power and authority to initiate cycles that may last forever.

If you find the point of balance anywhere in Cosmos,

you can travel unperturbed through the successive neutral centers all the way to the center of the Great Central Sun. All the centers of all the cycles are congruent in the highest dimension of Cosmos. Find one center and you have found them all. Find your first love and you have found all loves. Remain at the point of balance, of perfect love, and you reside in the heart of God.

This great secret pathway through the tunnels of cyclic equilibrium, designed into the fabric of life, is God's great gift to man. Become the dot in the center of his circle, correspond to the pulsation of his heart, and look forward to infinite horizons of beauty and perfectionment.

The Molding of Substance

The ancient wisdom teaches us that there is one element, one cosmic substance—*akasha*—from which all form is made. It is fluidic in motion, ethereal, and interpenetrates all substance. Without weight, without color of its own, it takes on the properties of vibratory patterns imposed upon it—patterns that can be impressed on it by sound and by thought.

Even Spirit has form. As we recede into the eternal depths of creation and rise into infinitely higher planes of consciousness, still there is form—and all conforms to the Law of Cycles.

All substance, all form, all life is the result of force causing Matter to move. *Force Causes Matter to Move.* Force can be generated voluntarily, consciously, by an intelligent being. The infinite hierarchy of ascended beings turns the wheels and cycles of worlds by the force of their will. Brahma uses force to mold galaxies. The Masters use force to mold ideas and create the various pockets of life in the universe.

> *"All of manifested Cosmos is the interplay of cyclic vibrations, initiated somewhere, somehow, by someone."*

Force can also be the impulse of the unconscious, meticulously accurate mechanism that drives the substratum of the material planes. Matter cannot be divorced from Spirit.

In order to have motion, there must be a medium through which vibrations can occur. The fluid nature of *akasha* responds to vibrational force in a wavelike, cyclic flow—just like the pebble thrown into the fluid pond. Motion is the alteration of *akasha* that is inherently in a state of harmony, of rest, of equilibrium. Apply any force into the ocean of *akasha* and cycles of motion result.

The myriad forms we see in the universe are the conglomerate wave patterns resulting from simple or complex combinations of sine waves moving in cycles. The days and nights of Brahma, if symbolized in two dimensions, would be an even, rhythmic flow between the two poles of the cosmic magnet. The allness of the one element is driven into motion by the will of God.

Scientists Douglas Vogt and Gary Sultan have approached the inner workings of this Law of Cycles. They postulate in their book *Reality Revealed* that all of the physical elements are brought into our plane by the interaction of cyclic waveforms. The simplest form of motion is represented by the sine wave. This diagram represents sine waves interacting in two planes of angular dimension.

Science and the Laya Center

The conception of the Ascended Masters is, of course, complete, whereas few scientists have penetrated the mystery of the point of balance, the *laya center*. Nikola Tesla found

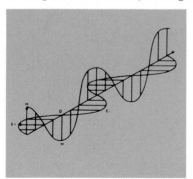

the power at the neutral center of all cycles—and proceeded to conceptualize devices that would perpetually run on the cyclic vibrations of our planetary sphere as it pulsates with a heartbeat of its own. Unfortunately for us, Tesla's motor was never developed for public use.

Tesla was not the only one who discovered the power at the center of the circle. One of the greatest scientists of all time, ironically unknown to our modern clan of quark-seekers, was Mr. John Worrell Keely of Philadelphia.

Quoted in *The Secret Doctrine* of H. P. Blavatsky, in explanation of an engine he designed, Mr. Keely says:

*In the conception of any machine heretofore con-
structed, the medium for inducing a neutral center
has never been found. If it had, the difficulties
of perpetual-motion seekers would have ended, and
this problem would have become an established and
operating fact. It would only require an introductory
impulse of a few pounds, on such a device, to cause it
to run for centuries. In the conception of my vibratory
engine, I did not seek to attain perpetual motion; but
a circuit is formed that actually has a neutral center,
which is in a condition to be vivified by my vibratory
ether, and, while under operation by said substance,
is really a machine that is virtually independent of
the mass (or globe), and it is the wonderful velocity
of the vibratory circuit that makes it so.*

*Still, with all its perfection, it requires to be fed
with the vibratory ether to make it an independent
motor. . . . .All structures require a foundation in strength
according to the weight of the mass they have to carry,
but the foundations of the universe rest on a vacuous
point far more minute than a molecule; in fact, to
express this truth properly, on an inter-etheric point,
which requires an infinite mind to understand it.*

*To look down into the depths of an etheric center
is precisely the same as it would be to search into the
broad space of heaven's ether to find the end, with this
difference: that one is the positive field, while the
other is the negative field.*

We have here the marriage of the science of Matter
with the laws of Spirit. This etheric neutral point, balanced
between the positive and negative, is the dot suspended in the
center of the circle of God's being.

The Point of Peace

As man evolves through the folds of time and space, the
key to safe passage through the initiatic tests is harmony and
balance. The vicissitudes of life can all be viewed objectively
from the balance point in the center of our heart, which is
congruent with the center of God's heart. We can move through
all cycles and not be removed from this stable point if we but
apply this science of cycles.

To illustrate this, visualize an ordinary seesaw in a playground. It is a flat board resting on a central pivot point. As a child mounts on each end of the board, they create a cyclic movement that would look like a sine wave if represented in a graph. But notice that the center of the board, the center of the cycle, is absolutely stationary. The children can be moving wildly, frantically on the ends, and the center is always balanced and stable.

Thus it is with all cycles, and thus it can be through all of life. This cyclic center in man is the heart chakra.

The body of man is a magnet. This has been proven by scientists and spiritual healers alike. We recall that all magnets create cycles of positive and negative flow. The heart is that point of equilibrium of the flow of prana through our system. There is a place of perfect harmony in the secret chamber of the heart, which is beyond the physical heart, pulsating in cyclic rhythm seventy-two times a minute every day of our lives.

This is why the Masters tell us to go there, to go to this point of balance in our hearts. Because there is the point of peace. But it is also the point of power.

Return through the Word

The path of the ascension is the means whereby sons of God preserve an identity as a single cell in the being of Brahma throughout the *pralayas* and throughout the inhalation and the exhalation of God.

As we noted earlier, in each *yuga*, man is given specific spiritual tools to assist him in his evolution.

It is said that we are presently in a *Kali Yuga*—a cycle of returning karma, the darkest of all four of the cycles. Sanat Kumara, the Great Guru, assigns forms of communion with God that are befitting the evolutions of man within the *yugas*.

Sanat Kumara has told us that in this *yuga*, the key to contact God is the science of the spoken Word. Using this science, practiced by adepts East and West for thousands of years, we can send forth auric emanations from the point of power within the center of our heart to heal our personal microcosm and the world outside the boundary of our skin.

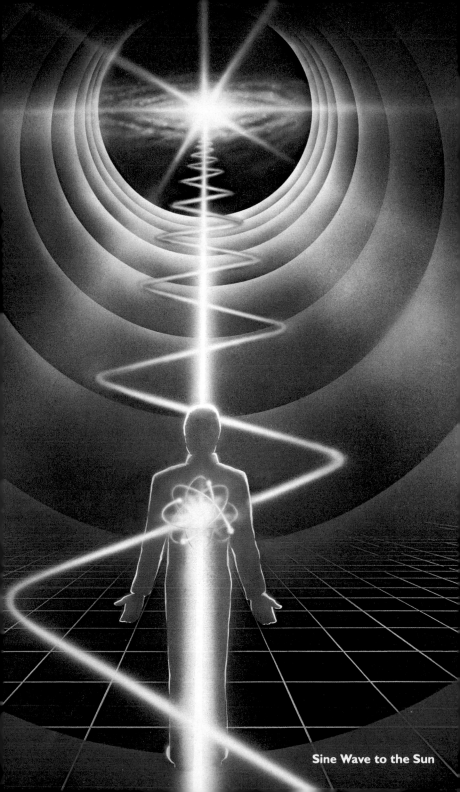

Sine Wave to the Sun

To endure as a cell in the consciousness of God when that God is at perfect rest is to enter with him into the cosmic cycle of nirvana. To do this, one must pass through the nexus of the cycle—the Word.

The eternal Logos is the dot in the center of the circle, the beginning and ending of cycles that are composed of circles, layer upon layer.

In the beginning was Brahma, and the Word was with Brahma, and the Word was with Brahma in the beginning. Therefore, in order to be in Brahma, we must be in the Word. "No man cometh to the Father but by me." That "me" is the supreme I AM THAT I AM manifest as the Word.

It is a swaddling garment wound around about the earth. The very currents of the earth's surface, the very emanations from its sun center, the Law of Cycles, the comfort flame, the hum just below the level of our own hearing transfers to us this comfort of the cyclic law of the sounding of God's Word.

Life is ongoing, and the Law of Cycles promises us that life will go on. God's heart will beat on. The wheel of cyclic return will rotate on the spokes of our karmic creations.

By the Law of Cycles, then, we are set upon our courses spiraling through once again the nexus of being, the nexus being the Word itself, the Law of Cycles being the emanation of the Word. As we become congruent with the dot in the center of God's circle, the power is bestowed upon us to imprint the cyclic energies of God with the pattern of our God-oriented idea or desire.

This is the way to return to God as a permanent atom in his being—through this Word that has incarnated in the avatars with the cyclic law of manifestation. The great *Manus*, the Lawgivers of the ages and of their races, upheld the cycle of the Word whereby all seed going forth from the great Tree of Life might return through the Word as the Law of Cycles.

There is joy in this Law of Cycles. And the joy of this marriage of science and religion is you at the nexus of infinity, you converging with that living Word.

Your Divine Self

The Chart of Your Divine Self

There are three figures represented in the Chart, which we will refer to as the upper figure, the middle figure, and the lower figure.

The upper figure is the I AM Presence, the I AM THAT I AM, the individualization of God's presence for every son and daughter of the Most High.

The Divine Monad consists of the I AM Presence surrounded by the spheres (color rings) of light which comprise the causal body. This is the body of First Cause that contains within it man's "treasure laid up in heaven" — words and works, thoughts and feelings of virtue, attainment, and light — pure energies of love that have risen from the plane of action in time and space as the result of man's judicious exercise of free will and his harmonious qualification of the stream of life that issues forth from the heart of the Presence and descends to the level of the Christ Self, thence to invigorate and enliven the embodied soul.

The middle figure in the Chart is the Mediator between God and man, called the Holy Christ Self, the Real Self, or the Christ consciousness. It has also been referred to as the Higher Mental Body or one's Higher Consciousness.

This Inner Teacher overshadows the lower self, which consists of the soul evolving through the four planes of Matter using the vehicles of the four lower bodies (the etheric, or memory, body; the mental body; the emotional, or desire, body; and the physical body) to balance karma and fulfill the divine plan.

The three figures of the Chart correspond to the Trinity of Father (the upper figure), Son (the middle figure), and Holy Spirit (the lower figure). The latter is the intended temple of the Holy Spirit, whose sacred fire is indicated in the enfolding violet flame. The lower figure corresponds to you as a disciple on the Path. Your soul is the nonpermanent aspect of being which is made permanent through the ritual of the ascension. The ascension is the process whereby the soul, having balanced her karma and fulfilled her divine plan, merges first with the Christ consciousness and then with the living Presence of the I AM THAT I AM. Once the ascension has taken place, the soul, the nonpermanent aspect of being, becomes the Incorruptible One, a permanent atom in the Body of God. The Chart of Your Divine Self is therefore a diagram of yourself — past, present, and future.

The lower figure represents the son of man or child of the Light evolving beneath his own 'Tree of Life'. This is how you should visualize yourself standing in the violet flame, which you invoke daily in the name of the I AM Presence and your Holy Christ Self in order to purify your four lower bodies in preparation for the ritual of the alchemical marriage — your soul's union with the Beloved, your Holy Christ Self.

The lower figure is surrounded by a tube of light, which is projected from the heart of the I AM Presence in answer to your call. It is a cylinder of white light which sustains a forcefield of protection 24 hours a day, so long as you guard it in harmony. It is also invoked daily with the "Heart, Head, and Hand Decrees" and may be reinforced as needed.

The threefold flame of Life is the divine spark sent from the I AM Presence as the gift of life, consciousness, and free will. It is sealed in the secret chamber of the heart that through the Love, Wisdom and Power of the Godhead anchored therein the soul may fulfill her reason for being in the physical plane. Also called the Christ flame and the liberty flame, or fleur-de-lis, it is the spark of a man's Divinity, his potential for Christhood.

The silver (or crystal) cord is the stream of life, or "lifestream," that descends from the heart of the I AM Presence to the Holy Christ Self to nourish and sustain (through the chakras) the soul and its vehicles of expression in time and space. It is over this 'umbilical' cord that the energy of the Presence flows, entering the being of man at the crown and giving impetus for the pulsation of the threefold flame as well as the physical heartbeat. When a round of the soul's incarnation in Matter-form is finished, the I AM Presence withdraws the silver cord, whereupon the threefold flame returns to the level of the Christ, and the soul clothed in the etheric garment gravitates to the highest level of her attainment where she is schooled between embodiments, until her final incarnation when the great law decrees she shall go out no more.

The dove of the Holy Spirit descending from the heart of the Father is shown just above the head of the Christ. When the son of man puts on and becomes the Christ consciousness as Jesus did, he merges with the Holy Christ Self. The Holy Spirit is upon him and the words of the Father, the beloved I AM Presence, are spoken, "This is my beloved Son in whom I AM well pleased" (Matt. 3:17).

A more detailed explanation of the Chart of Your Divine Self is given in *The Lost Teachings of Jesus* and *Climb the Highest Mountain* by the Prophets.

A Shepherd Boy Contemplates the Riddle of Existence

Communication/Contemplation

for your Taurus initiation on the path of the Heart ♉

chapter five
part one

*Continuity
of
communication
with the Center
of all Life...*

*... through
        communication of
                my heart
        with the larger Heart
of which I am a part.*

Friends Who Love to Do His Will,

I am reminded of an experience which I had long ago in an incarnation little known by me prior to my ascension. It was in the Middle East where I was embodied in the Arab world as a shepherd keeping watch over the flocks charged to my care in what are now the Syrian foothills.

One night as I lay out in the open gazing at the stars, in contemplating the oneness of Life which I felt even then as a current that traversed the skies and then descended in an arc to be anchored in my heart—I heard the sound of horses and saw a group of foreigners approaching.

My soul told me that they were not of the light. And there was a restlessness that swept across the sheep. We were aware at once of a foreboding of evil.

As the caravan of horses drew nigh, I sought to hide myself with the sheep—but to no avail. The men signaled me to draw nigh.

The vibration of their evil consciousness intensified moment by moment. Was it my destiny to encounter this forcefield of blackness generated by the rebellion of laggard souls? Was it karma? Was it opportunity? Or both?

In my shepherd's robe and with my crook, I walked toward them in moments that seemed an eternity. As I approached their band, I saw that they were robbers with a booty of stolen goods— horses, gold, jewels, and silks (I was to find out later).

One among them, the leader of the band, eyed me with a penetrating gaze. And then he spoke in my native tongue, "Shepherd boy, come hither."

He said: "We are of your
native village and we come from the
highway of Damascus. We are
being pursued by a rival band of
outlaws and have need of a hiding
place for our stolen goods. You
must take them from us and hold
them in a nearby cave until our
return, for we must deal with this
rival band and eliminate them as
quickly as possible. If you do not
perform as we have demanded, we
will see to it that great harm comes
to your family."

Terrified yet composed, I saw
that I had no alternative but to
consent for the moment to the
demands of the brigands.

I showed them a hiding place
in an out-of-the-way cave. The
goods were transported there. And
they made their exit as quickly as
they had come—leaving me to
contemplate once again the riddle of
existence.

In my soul I knew that I must
protect my family, yet I also knew
that it was wrong to harbor evil
or to give sanctuary to the evil ones.
And I prayed to God as the Spirit
of Nature, as the abiding presence

of the Holy Spirit whom I knew not according to theology but according to the communication of my heart with the larger Heart of which I was a part.

Not six hours passed before the rival band of outlaws could be seen moving as a cloud of dust approaching nearer and nearer the place where I was tending sheep—a pass in the hills often used by travelers from the North.

In my musings of the hours as I called upon the Lord in my quandary, the thought waves which came upon me as comfort from the mind of God echoed the statement found in sacred Scripture "Vengeance is mine; I will repay, saith the Lord."[1]

I was comforted with the sense of cosmic justice. There is a reason, I said to myself, why this has happened to me. It is a challenge and a chance to know more of Him.

I will wait upon the Lord beside the flowing stream and learn his ways. I will not preempt the Lord, but I will allow him to perform his perfect work in me.

Thus as the second band of

dark ones approached, I was in a
frame of consciousness to extend
welcome to them who would be
instruments for the outpicturing of
judgment and of balance, which I
knew in my soul to be the law of
the universe.

It was thus that I sat meditating
under a tree on that night so clearly
lit by the moon's reflection of the
solar orb. They stopped at my
resting place, and their leader
questioned me concerning the
whereabouts of the previous
outlaws.

I said that I did not know if
they had come through in the
previous day, for I had not seen
them. And after a pause beside the
stream, they journeyed on down
into the valley in the direction taken
by the other band. And the last I
saw of them, they disappeared
around some boulders that lined the
descending path.

Time passed—days, then
weeks—and there was no word from
either of them. I was no longer
anxious, for my trust was in Him
whose gentle radiance hung in the
very air as the swaddling garment

of an all-pervading Spirit reaching out to care for humanity and elemental life.

I dwelled in the comfort flame in that life much in the same manner that the Maha Chohan, the Representative of the Holy Spirit, tarried in that flame in India, keeping the flame for untold millions as a shepherd on the hillsides. And as you know, Kahlil Gibran was also embodied as a shepherd boy in the Middle East.

And thus God provides incarnations for the soul providing the simple way of nature, the joy of communion, and an absence of responsibility to the things of this world that makes for continuity of communication with other planes, with cosmic beings, and with the center of all Life—the very flame of God itself.

By and by there came to me news from the valley through the shepherds bringing their flocks to greener pastures for the summer.

They talked of nothing but the battle of the bands of robbers who had a confrontation not many miles from my native village and who by

their vengeance tore one another
limb from limb until no man
remained from among them to tell
the story but only young boys
playing in the rocks who hid at the
sound of their furious fight and
watched the battle to the end and
then ran to tell the townsfolk.

Once the dust had settled and
people had begun to analyze in
their way the events that had
transpired, they concluded that the
fight must have been over stolen
goods. But all were perplexed, for
no goods had been found.

I listened and I smiled. And I
bade the shepherds on their way.

And when even came, I prayed
to my God: "O Lord, these goods
are not mine, but thine. They have
come forth out of this universe, out
of this flaming Presence which I
know to be yourself. I reclaim them
for thee. And yet I would return
them to those merchants who lost
them at the hand of the robbers.
Yet how can I, a poor shepherd,
leave my flocks to go in search of
whom I know not? And then what
am I to say? For whoever I ask will
claim them for his own."

Again the ripples of joy that come from the source of Life inundated the shores of my being. And I felt the indwelling Presence and the "Peace, be still" and the "All is well" consciousness.[2] For the communication of God was to my heart a communication beyond words, even beyond the formulation of mental or verbal concepts.

In my childlike acceptance of the Creator and myself as one of his creatures, humble yet aware of a cosmic purpose being worked out in my life, I knew that the Lord would deliver me from the burden of the stolen goods.

One day I went to the cave to examine the contents in the cache—beautiful silks, spices, gold coins and golden jewelry, and precious stones that I had not seen before. I was aware from the vibration of the goods themselves that these would be precious in the markets of the world.

But of what value were they to me who had all of God in health, in joy, in the service of Life which was my calling? And then I thought of the needs of my family and the children in the village and what all of this could provide for them to increase their opportunity to find that oneness with Life which I already knew.

In next week's Pearl, I shall continue the unfoldment of my story taken directly from the records of akasha.[3]

Lanello

The Foreverness
of Love

Transformation/Ministration

for your Taurus initiation on the path of the Heart ♉

chapter five
part two

Selfless acts
are seeds
planted
in the soul
of a planet...

...a compelling
momentum
for Love
as the foundation
of a new age.

Friends Who Love and Continue
to Love to Do His Will,

Taking up again the spiral of
my experience in the Middle East, I
give you the conclusion of this most
unusual episode of my lifestream.

The weeks passed into months,
the months into the turning of the
year. And Life continually revealed
itself to me in nature.

One day as I was tending the
sheep, I saw a caravan approaching
in the distance, which was not
unusual for this time of year. For
many merchants came through this
country on the way to Damascus to
sell their wares. As the company

drew nigh, they stopped to refresh themselves at my camp.

As I had a stew brewing on the fire, I invited them to partake of my humble fare. For to me, whether rich man, beggar, or thief—all came forth from the one God, hence all were brothers.

They accepted my hospitality. And as the meal progressed, they began to recount the tales of their many journeys.

And then they spoke of having been accosted by a band of robbers many months before, of having been stripped of their goods and several members of their party murdered. I asked them to describe what had been stolen from them, and they went to great length to give me the details of the silks and jewels and gold that I knew only too well.

When I was convinced that these were indeed the ones who had lost the goods which I was holding in the cave, I invited them to come up with me to the hiding place. As we climbed the rocks, I unwound the tale of my adventure and I told them of the fate of the bands of robbers.

When they saw their treasure intact before their very eyes, they could not believe it. How great their joy! How great their gratitude!

They turned to me and they said: "O shepherd of the hills, your honesty is greater than any we have ever seen. If all men were like you, what a different life it would be—what a different world!"

Had they left with all that was theirs, I would have been grateful simply for the opportunity to balance Life's energies—to right a wrong that had been done. But they did not.

They gave to me one third of all that was there, insisting that I take it for myself. But I said: "Alas, I am happy as a shepherd. I will see to it that conditions are improved for my people in the village. And we will dig a well and provide care for the needy and give assistance to the poor." They were astounded when they learned of my wishes and that I desired nothing for myself, so much so that they offered their help to implement a plan on behalf of my people.

I tell you this story—an episode in a lifetime, a lifetime among many—because of the record that was left in akasha there in the hillsides where these events transpired and of a flame of the Holy Spirit that was anchored there because love was born and kindled in the hearts of one and a few.

Many centuries have gone by since those precious hours of my communion with God. But as I look down the years and see the events that have transpired since, I note with joy that all who have passed that way have also been kindled with love, with concern for their fellowman. And the events that have flowed from that beginning have turned the tide in many souls, in many hearts.

Some who come and are weary, others who are vicious and dark, as they approach the place where virtue is enshrined, find lofty thoughts, aspiration, and concern for humanity beginning to dawn upon the consciousness. They are refreshed in a spiritual way. And they do not leave that place without receiving in some measure the transforming energies which love does impart.

By putting on the garment of the Lord, by putting on his consciousness, his awareness of Life forms, and loving the many parts of the Whole as one, I was able to pave the way for others—perhaps to touch the hem of that garment, perhaps to be impressed with the jewellike virtues embroidered thereon.

And in conclusion may I say that everyone who has ever passed that place has received something (even the most hardened) in some degree, however small, by the actions of those days—by the integration of my soul with the souls of total strangers who by rendering mutual service implanted the signet of Genesis "I AM my brother's keeper."[4]

I have recounted this to you that you might go and do likewise—that you might render service, knowing that every act that is selfless is a seed that is planted in the soul of a planet and that that seed will mature and wax strong and then blossom as a floral adornment for those who come after.

This is the meaning of the blooming of Aaron's rod.[5] When man and woman use the energies of the sacred fire—the rod of power that flows from the heart on the altar of the spine—in service and devotion to one another and to all mankind, they find the blossoming in their own world of the virtues which they have planted and watered and which God has increased.[6]

And all who pass in the way where you walk where you have left the record of selflessness will likewise be impelled to perpetuate that spiral which you have initiated. And, by and by, the reinforcement of virtue by successive acts multiplied by other acts builds a compelling momentum for love as the foundation of a new civilization, a new age, and a new hierarchy.

Life will not resist the flow toward the source of love. For all of life, great and small, in the very core of being desires to reunite with the flame of love.

To put on the garment of the

Lord, you must first divest yourself
of resistance to this flow, to this
love, and then demonstrate in small
deeds as well as great ones that
yours is a living faith—a faith of
action that is realized word by
word, deed by deed.

Then you will see the hope of
mankind gain new fervor because
you have set the example. Then you
will see how charity begets charity
and how the community of the
Holy Spirit is fashioned anew out of
flame flowers that have become one
in the thousand-petaled lotus of the
Buddhic light.

I shall speak to you again of
the foreverness of love.

Lanello

Unclean Spirits Challenge the Sane and the Insane

Unification/Affinitization

for your Gemini initiation on the path of the Heart **II**

chapter six

*Life must obey
the Law of Cycles,
atomic particles
must come
into alignment
with true Being...*

*... And that which
is of the Light
must confirm Light
while that which
is of darkness
must confirm darkness.*

Devotees of the Light of God,

Are you beflamed by the majesty of His will as I am? Are you seized with a passion that is the love of God? Does your heart burn in the anticipation of His presence and do you yearn to be filled with the wisdom of His law?

If for you life is but an encounter with obstacles that heighten the homeward race and that fill you with anticipation just to see His face—then come with me as I extol the virtues of oneness and as I lay before you the knowledge of the law, the awareness of the bliss of love, and as I show you how to

pursue wholeness, to defend
oneness, and in being God how to
remain undefiled, uncontaminated
by the world.

The path of discipleship is a
path that leads the soul gently from
a consciousness of duality to the
consciousness of unity, of oneness
in the white-fire core of being.

Successive stages of initiation
of the unfoldment of the mind of
God within the mind of man are for
the putting off of the old man and
the putting on of the new.[1] These
are for the release of the veils of
duality, of mortality, and their
replacement with the garment of the
Lord—the seamless garment of grace
and light's effulgence.[2]

Day by day, the Lord leadeth
the children of promise out of the
land of bondage, across the desert—
parting the turbulent sea, clearing
the path to summit heights where
the vision of the promised land
is seen by the elect of God who have
kept the vision of oneness.

Those who perceive oneness
have the right to conceive oneness
and to bring it forth from out the
white-fire core in the planes of

Spirit into the planes of Mater.

Each step of the way, challenges arise. Each bend in the road is a mark of attainment that precipitates the precipice of challenge.

In chaos and chimera, by the flame of wholeness, scattered energies are drawn into rods of power, erratic movements become dynamic momentums, and jagged emotions are geometrized as a cone of self-realization.

Every phase of maya, every phantom of the mist is resolved, even as dissonant sound by the law of truth becomes the orchestration of celestial harmonics.

By meditation upon the Christic light, by the converging of self-consciousness with God Self-consciousness, man and woman putting on the garment of the Lord become one in the spiral of our oneness.

When Jesus came into the country of the Gadarenes, he was met by one who came out of the tombs, a man with an unclean spirit who could not be bound—no, not with chains. Nor could he be tamed but was found always night and day in the mountains and in the tombs, crying and cutting himself with stones. But when he saw Jesus from afar off, he ran and worshiped him.[3]

The record of Christ's healing of this one possessed of an unclean spirit is written clearly in akasha. It is the record of an illusion of duality, a manifestation that confounded all the people of that country and which still confounds the scientists and the doctors two thousand years after this healing that was brought about by the Spirit and in the power of the Lord.

The infestation of the sheaths of consciousness that surround the soul as a swaddling garment has occurred since the hour when man and woman rejected the wholeness of God and elected by the misuse of free will to separate themselves from the twin flames of sacred fire in the center of being.

The sheaths of consciousness which surround the soul we call the four lower bodies. These are the vehicles of the soul's expression and expansion in the plane of Mater. They are the *etheric* or *memory body,* the *mental body,* the *emotional* or *astral body,* and the *physical body.* Through these interpenetrating forcefields, the soul projects the energies of Spirit into manifestation in the world of Matter form.

Here the soul gains experience in the manipulation of the laws governing time and space. Here the soul proves self-mastery by working the works of God in man. And thus he obeys the injunction of the Lord "Take dominion over the earth."[4]

Sacred vessels are these four bodies of man, of woman—yea, even the habitation of the Most High God.[5]

But when the vision of oneness descends to the level of relativity in Matter, engendering a sense of separation from the central flame of Life, then the door of consciousness is opened not to the Christ but to the dweller on the threshold and to the fallen ones—discarnates, demons, and entities who seek a dwelling place in the tabernacle of God that has become the tomb of the living dead.

Now we see in the one who is marked by society as insane only

the extreme manifestation of what
those who are sane experience as
the parallel manifestation of the
Christ mind and the carnal mind
side by side in the evolving
soul-consciousness.

The insane are those who are
not able to resolve patterns of
duality and to live a normal life
while tolerating that warring within
the members of which Paul spoke.[6]
The insane are those who have been
split in two—mind and heart, body
and soul being utterly rent in twain
by the manifestation simultaneously
of that which is one with the Christ
on the one hand and that which
is aligned with evil and the devil on
the other.

Those who remain sane, then,
are those who have the ability to
tolerate within the four lower
bodies at once the elements of the
old man that is being put off and of
the new man that is being put on.

There are times when those
who are sane do pass through
periods of insanity. These periods
of emotional turmoil take place as
the soul for a period of hours or
days is unable to come to grips with

the forces of light and darkness as these are embattled for the victory of the domain of consciousness. Likewise, there are periods when the so-called insane resolve the clashing and the clamoring of forces and are found to be passive if not wholly rational for indefinite periods.

The duality of this one with an unclean spirit is seen as his soul and his heart run to greet the Christ, the Saviour, and to worship him, acknowledging him as the source of salvation and of freedom from bondage while at the same time the unclean spirit dwelling within the recesses of the mental and emotional bodies cries out with a loud voice, saying: "What have I to do with thee, Jesus, thou Son of the Most High God? I adjure thee by God that thou torment me not."

The fiat of the Christ "Come out of the man, thou unclean spirit" is the commanding presence of the Word, of the Logos itself, by which the creation was framed.[7] Jesus, being filled with the Holy Ghost and being imbued with the action of the law, must exact obedience from all that which comes in contact with his flame.

Wherever he is, life must obey the law of cycles, atomic particles must come into alignment with true being, and that which is of the light must confirm the light while that which is of darkness must confirm darkness. And the definition of that which is Real and that which is unreal is clearly seen in the presence of the Christ as the action of the sacred Word—the *sword* that cleaves asunder the True Self from the not-self.

Aside from the compassionate Christ Presence which he exemplified, Jesus was the fullness of the expression of the law. The unclean spirit did not belong in the house of God. The unclean spirit was not in its proper place. By the law of harmony, by the law of the wholeness of Alpha and Omega in the very center of the heart flame of the Christ, energies must be resolved to their proper planes.

And thus Jesus asks, "What is thy name?" For by pronouncing the name (which is the key to the vibration, to the electronic forcefield,

of the entity) Jesus will key the
energies of the Holy Spirit to that
frequency for the removal of that
force, that disquieting factor which
has no part with the architecture
of the cosmic cube—the real identity
of man. And he answered, saying,
"My name is Legion: for we are
many."

And the unclean spirit
besought Jesus that he would not
send them away, that he would not
send this legion of discarnates out
of the country—the place of the
familiar. These discarnates, which
scriptures record as being devils,
besought Jesus, saying: "Send us
into the swine, that we may enter
into them," for there was nigh unto
the mountains a great herd of swine
feeding. Their request shows that in
the presence of the Christ they also
desired to return to that level of
awareness, that vibration, kindred to
their own on the astral plane.

The swine consciousness was
that to which in reality they were
affinitized. By the law of affinity of
vibration, therefore, Jesus gave them
leave. And they went out of the
man and entered into the swine.

And yet that phase of elemental life that retained God-awareness, even within the swine, refused to submit to the lower aspect of their nature which the unclean spirits personified. And thus their consciousness being split, the group soul of the swine preferred to reunite with the Spirit of God in nature than to remain in the presence of the discarnates. And so they ran violently down a steep place into the sea (they were about two thousand) and were choked in the sea.

Now and then in the history of the evolution of elemental life through the animal kingdom, there have been recorded incidences where elementals desiring to be released from the burden and the weight of an astral force that has overtaken the animal consciousness have sacrificed themselves in great numbers, thereby sharing in the sacrifice of Jesus the Christ on behalf of the balance of harmony in the planet and in all mankind.

This, then, is the teaching of the Brotherhood on the putting on of the garment of the Lord through a return to wholeness. I shall return in the next Pearl of Wisdom to the subject of wholeness and the reunification of man and woman in the flame of the One.

I AM shining in the brightness of immortal spheres.

I AM your
Lanello

The Symmetry
of the Fourfold
Consciousness of God

Integration/Polarization

for your Cancer initiation on the path of the Heart ♋

chapter seven

*The prominence of
the Divine Mother
in the
Aquarian Age
necessitates a restoration...*

...of precious energies
of the Holy Ghost
in mind and soul,
in heart
and in body temple.

To Those Who Espouse the Flames
   of Alpha and Omega as the
   Father/Mother God,

   "The fining pot is for silver,
and the furnace for gold: but the
Lord trieth the hearts."[1]
   As we contemplate methods
of self-realization through the
reunification of man and woman in
the flame of the One, let us consider
now how nature is the backdrop
for the return to wholeness that
comes about as man and woman,
representing the twin flames of the
Paraclete, unite their energies in
devotion to the common cause of
the betterment of life on Terra.

The wholeness of God
expressed in nature—released
through flora and fauna, through
the giant hills and snowy summits,
the vastness of the plains and
the tides of the sea—conveys to
humanity the consciousness of God
in all of its aspects.

Standing upon the shore of
life contemplating the mystery
of oneness, man and woman bear
witness to the planes of God's
consciousness in the fire of
the sun, in the currents of the
air caressing all life, and in the
movement of the waters lapping
the shore of Mother earth.

Thus the four lower bodies
of a planet are seen as dimensions
of consciousness which may be
penetrated at will by man and
woman who seek to know God in
the fusion of their heart flames and
the merging of Alpha and Omega
spirals for the victory of noble
endeavor, their sacred labor—most
cherished creation.

The sun reminds the soul of
its ancient heritage in the white-fire
core of being where twin flames
were born and danced to the

rhythm of the heartbeat of God. The sphere of golden-pink glow ray suspended in space holds the blueprint of cosmic destiny and the geometry of an origin far, far beyond the ken of mortal knowing.

From the fiery ovoid in the heart of the Presence—the I AM THAT I AM—Life delivered unto life a polarity of consciousness: "male and female created he them."[2] Thus the I AM Presence of twin flames, through the fission of the white-fire core, became a dual manifestation out of which twin souls descended to take dominion in the four planes of Mater.

The rays of the sun, the Life-giving essence of eternity, stir the ashes on the grate of consciousness, stir the memory of far-off worlds. And souls basking in the summer sunlight know that sometime, somewhere, all shall return to the fiery womb of creation and to the reunion of twin flames.

Thus the fire body of man, of planets, and of stars is the etheric (or memory) sheath in which are etched in fiery crystal the memory and the design of other spheres

of opportunity, other worlds
of consciousness. Through self-
mastery, the disciplines of the law,
and the initiations of hierarchy,
these designs can be precipitated in
the plane of Mater for the victory
of a flame called love.

In the plane of air, a
transparency for fire, water, and
earth—invisible like the wind that
"bloweth where it listeth"[3]—is seen
the coming of the Holy Spirit as the
completeness of Alpha and Omega
spirals that in each holy child
become the breath of Life. In air,
every duality is resolved into
oneness by the Father/Mother God.

And thus it is the plane of the
mind—of that Christ mind which
was in Christ Jesus which is clear
thinking, clear seeing, sound logic,
and conceptual purity when
unencumbered by the pollutants of
the carnal mind. Just as the
atmosphere is burdened by the
smog of mankind's abuse of the
sacred energies and resources of
Life, so the mental belt is sundered
by the profanity and the insanity of
mortal pride.

Yet here purely do the winds

of the Holy Spirit create the transition from fire to water. Air is the medium wherein the flow of cosmic energy is seen in the precipitation of water to the earth below.

Thus it is that through the Mediator of the Christ mind, the fiery energies of the Father are transferred as a mighty flow that becomes the love of the Mother for the whole of creation.

Thus into the plane of water, reflecting the desire body of the Father/Mother, there are transferred from higher planes of the Alpha-to-Omega consciousness the exalted feelings of God for the creation. And water as energy-in-motion in man and in woman is a conductor of the energies of Life and all of the ingredients that are necessary to the nourishment of the soul and its faculties.

The minerals that nourish plant life are transferred by water. And the body temples of elementals and mankind are made up almost entirely of this Mother flow. The physical plane, the earth body and the earth earthy[4] of Mother earth, is the detail of God's cosmic consciousness transferred to atoms and molecules, etching in Matter form all of the wondrous designs that originate in the white-fire core of the central sun.

Now as the symmetry of the fourfold consciousness of God is related to the evolving consciousness of man and woman, we perceive the law of integration whereby man is intended to personify the attributes of Father and Son as these relate to the planes of fire and air, and woman is intended to personify the attributes of Mother and Holy Spirit as these relate to the planes of water and earth.

In this, the wholeness of the sphere of the Father/Mother God becomes twain for the purpose of evolution and for the realization of the Holy Spirit through twin souls who come forth out of the white-fire core of being.

In every particle of Matter, in every design of nature, there is seen the infinite beauty of this polarity of the positive and negative spirals of the Godhead.

In the table of elements and precious metals and gems, in the endless varieties of plant life and all of the inventions of which mankind has conceived and which he has derived from the mind of God—there is to be seen the yin and the yang of the Divine Whole.

"The fining pot is for silver, and the furnace for gold: but the Lord trieth the hearts."

So is gold the focus of Alpha energies and silver the repository of the frequencies of Omega. And the Lord Christ who trieth the hearts is the individual Christ Self who releases the energies of the Logos into the hearts of mankind to see whether they are able to retain the elements of grace, of virtue and nobility which enable man and woman to outpicture the Christ consciousness and the balanced threefold flame.

Now then, all that divides—all that seeks to tear down the glorious manifestation of the fourfold nature of God as his consciousness must manifest in man and in woman—is not of the light but of the darkness.

The divide-and-conquer tactics

of the Luciferians, the fallen ones, and their ploys are abroad in the land. And in this hour of the Dark Cycle[5] of Gemini (which began April 23, 1974, and will continue until April 23, 1975) there is almost a relentless siege by the demons of the night to discredit every noble endeavor, every family, hearth, and home, and even the individual by causing schism, the splitting of the personality, the dividing of loved ones through argumentation, dissension, envy, jealousy, and turbulent emotional energies.

Therefore, in my instruction which I am releasing in these Pearls of Wisdom on putting on the garment of the Lord, I cannot fail to admonish you to seek the flame of wholeness through the getting of the Holy Spirit.

The pursuit of the Holy Spirit is for some Christian groups the all and end of existence. And with a love and a fervor that sometimes consume their entire beings, they wait upon the coming of the Lord as the indwelling presence of the Comforter.

Those who are students of

ascended master law need not feel
that this pursuit is set aside alone
for those who call themselves
Christians. For you who have
perceived the higher criticism of the
law and the inner teachings of the
Christ must also recognize that the
coming into prominence in the
Aquarian age of the Divine Mother
necessitates the restoration of the
precious energies of the Holy Ghost
in mind and soul, in heart, and in
body temple.

Each of the four planes of
consciousness, each of the
four lower bodies, must become the
dwelling place of the Most High God.

And many of you have reached
a point in your application of the
sacred fire and in your invocations
where you can now call upon
the name of the Lord as the
I AM THAT I AM and give forth the
command to Life that the kingdom
of God come into manifestation, as
above so below, right within your
very being foursquare.

The Call to the Fire Breath
(see p. 264) is a call to the Holy Spirit
and should be given with persistence
by those who would entertain not

only angels unawares[6] but the very living, personal presence of the Maha Chohan himself.

You have heard in the dictation of Saint Germain which concluded the third quarter at the ascended masters' university that the Maha Chohan, the Representative of the Holy Spirit, will be the master teacher for third-quarter students. This dispensation of the Karmic Board and the hierarchy is not without purpose, nor was it made without careful consideration.

For in this age of a conquering of all—all darkness of the pit and the fierce energies of the Luciferians that try the souls of the elect—only the presence of the Holy Spirit, only the rushing of the mighty wind[7] in the being and consciousness of man and woman, can counteract the rising tide of nefarious negation and the astral sea that is the perversion of the Mother flow.

I leave you to your personal communion with the Holy Spirit and the recitation of the mantra to the fire breath until next week when we shall take up several important techniques for the magnetization of the flow of oneness from the center of that being which is the Holy Spirit.

I remain dedicated to the victorious fulfillment of the Father/Mother God in your life.

Lanello

The Flame
of the Holy Spirit

Magnification/Manifestation

for your Leo initiation on the path of the Heart ♌

chapter eight

*As you practice
the presence of Love,
the Christ of you
will draw nearer
and dearer
to your heart...*

*...until heaven
is realized on earth
and your aura,
an expanding egg
of cosmic consciousness,
merges with the aura
of the Christ.*

Hearts Who Would Be Filled
  with the Fires of the Holy Spirit,

I come to you in the flaming
presence of the Maha Chohan. For
we are one in the release of the
spoken Word presented to you
herewith as a Pearl of Wisdom from
our causal bodies.

As the Mother has taught her
children of the layers of the causal
body and likened them unto the
creation of the pearl by the oyster,
layer upon layer, so I would place
before you the awareness that your
causal body itself can be increased
as you magnify the Spirit of the
Lord by the Christ flame within

your heart. But first you must increase the corona of the flame of Life within your aura as you yourself employ the power of the spoken Word.

The flame of the Holy Spirit is a joyous flame, the soundless sound. It is the music of the spheres, the gentle rain, the foam that moves with the crest of the wave and mingles with the sand.

The flame of the Holy Spirit is the fresh, cool air that comes from the mountains at eventide.

The flame of the Holy Spirit is the love that burns within your heart when you meet a kindred soul along life's way and when you see the beauty of a child or a devotee kneeling in prayer. It is flame of Christ-illumination that fires the mind—that sparks creative thought and gives will to the imagination.

The Holy Spirit is the presence of the Father adorned by the love of the Mother nourishing Life in the newborn child.

Now, to know that Spirit and to have that flame, there must abide within you a love for your fellowman that is beyond all human

chicanery, all human involvement
and the sense of struggle that
makes mankind retreat to group
identification and the labeling
of friend and foe.

A love that can endure all
human commotion, betrayal, and
bartering for friendships, vying for
power, and even the competition of
egos is a love that perforce is not of
this world and yet can be drawn
into this world, into the arena of
action, to enfold life that is bereft of
comfort and even of contact with
the Presence on high.

The exercise of love is the
requirement of the hour. For love
must have strong sinews, a straight
spine, alertness of mind that comes
with the flow of energy from the
Presence of God to the heart of man
and through the four lower bodies.

Just as the talent that is unused
is lost and the skills of the physical
and mental bodies deteriorate
without exercise, so love itself must
be applied daily.

You need not wait for
the bubbling fountain of love to
overflow within your heart
to express your love for God in

manifestation. For the love that flows with spontaneity is the love that has been generated through habit—through habitually giving forth praise, honor, and gratitude to the Lord. Thus by priming the pump of the fount of love, you can be ready with that balm of Gilead on a moment's notice to soothe a weary heart, a tired body, or a soul in torment.

Love needs to be generated and regenerated. The more you send forth, the more you receive until your aura, as a giant egg, can increase in the brilliance and intensity of the pink fires of sunset and the warmth of hearth and home.

Love is the angel songs at twilight as the angels of the Maha Chohan make their daily spiral around the planet, assisting all to transfer the energies of the day into the hour of devotion to the Father/Mother God.

You can endow action, thought, word, and deed with an overlay of pink flame that will soften the authority of the will and temper the intensity of the mercurial mind.

When you lead with love
rather than with sarcasm or
resentment, when you give with
love rather than with conniving and
conceit, when you receive with love
rather than with hypocrisy, deceit,
or disdain—you endow material
substance, atoms and molecules,
and all in the family of God with a
tangible radiance of love that does
not fail to multiply and to gather
momentum.

You know that it is the practice
of many of the students to qualify
money with the fires of purification
and the cosmic honor flame. I say,
let the coin of the realm be
wrapped in love as you pay your
bills and give to those who serve
you that which is due the laborer
who is worthy of his hire.[1]

As you practice the presence of
love, you will find that the Christ of
you, your own Real Self, will draw
nearer and dearer to your heart. For
it is love in balance with wisdom
and power that enabled Jesus to
become the Christ and to be
accorded the appellation: Jesus,
the Christ.

Love draws the light of Father

and Son into balance. And love engenders a desire for greater and greater purity, even as it makes plain the necessity for personal sacrifice.

For to feel love is to desire to be that love. And to be that love is to continually transcend the former state until heaven is realized on earth and your aura, an expanding egg of cosmic consciousness, merges with the aura of the Christ and magnetizes so much more of your causal body into manifestation for the blessing of all mankind.

Through the crown chakra, the focus of the yellow ray, magnetize love in the love of the wisdom teachings.

Through the third-eye chakra, focus of the green ray, magnetize love by seeing the Cosmic Virgin as she enfolds all life in the immaculate conception—and go and do thou likewise.

Through the throat chakra, focus of the blue ray, magnetize love by the power of the spoken Word offered in praise of Father, Mother, Son, and Holy Spirit and by giving the adoration to the flame.

Through the heart, focus of the pink ray and the threefold flame, magnetize love as the adoration of the will of God, as the balance of the Christ mind, as the intuitive faculty of love itself, and as the wholeness of the Trinity in manifestation.

Through the solar plexus that is the focus of the ray of purple and gold, magnetize love by being thy brother's keeper and washing the feet of thy fellow servant on the Path.

Through the seat-of-the-soul chakra, focus of the violet ray, magnetize love in the pursuit of freedom, the invocation of mercy, and the upholding of justice.

Through the base-of-the-spine chakra, focus of the white ray of purity's light, magnetize love by the consecration of the energies of the sacred fire for the victory of the light in all of the chakras and for the restoration of purity at every level of consciousness.

Love, then, is a universal quality that is used as the action of the flame of the Holy Spirit to endow all of the rays—and the secret rays as well—with the magnetic impulse of God's love that is for the whole creation and that permeates that creation when it is intensified through the souls that He has made.

Now, before this course is complete we desire to have transferred to the devotees who are following our weekly releases an increment of the flame of the Holy Spirit as we merge our auras with your own.

And therefore we make known to you that we will stand, the Maha Chohan and myself, over each one who calls upon us. And we will place our mantle and the momentum of our causal bodies as an electronic forcefield over the four lower bodies of each devotee of the sacred fire who will call upon me as Lanello and upon the Maha Chohan as the Representative of the Holy Spirit.

This action of our consciousness enfiring your own can be made permanent only as you increase your application to the flame and pursue the high calling of the sons and daughters of God.

The calling which I deliver to you directly from the Great Initiator is this: to purify your chakras in this hour of the Lord's appearing.[2] For he would anchor his energies in the seven planes of consciousness—in the power of the seven rays released from the hearts of the mighty Elohim and their divine complements.

You must have not one but seven chalices prepared for the full complement of the Christ consciousness that must be delivered to some among mankind in this age to prepare the way for a higher order of evolved beings who are to appear on earth in the coming decades.

For, you see, as you prepare your temple as the dwelling place of the Holy Spirit, so the Holy Spirit prepares your temple to receive enlightened ones—avatars from far-off worlds and souls who have made considerable advancement evolving on Terra under the aegis of hierarchy.

For each sacrifice of human substance that is made by your free will, there is a corresponding release of divine substance into your being.

And therefore, although it
may be painful at times to rid
yourself of human momentums, of
carnal-mindedness, of involvement
with the interplay of egos and
the games that people play, and
although it takes a determined
will aligned with the will of the
Father to overcome momentums of
lethargy, complacency, rebellion,
and ego control—

Each victory that is won
Will replace your darkness with a sun
Of blazing glory in heart and mind,
Of star-fire light—
     'twill quicken all mankind!

Each morsel of substance
     you now revoke
Through light of prayer
     you do invoke
Will translate the human
     into the divine
And surely make your life sublime.

And so, my beloved,
     fear not the surrender,
Fear not the temptation
     or the blunder.
For the paltry energies
     that you give up
Will be returned as light
     to fill your cup.

Know, then, that the
   homeward path we view
Is a daily exchange—
   the human for the divine.
Do not fail to give Him his due,
And He will not fail to give thee thine.

Learn this, then, O chelas of Morya and Saint Germain—that to put on the consciousness of the Holy Spirit, you must put off the darkness and the profanity of the common man. You must be clothed in royal robes of king and priest, of son and daughter of God.

And therefore, if you would come to know Him whom I know as the very living presence of the cloven tongues of fire,[3] learn the discipline of self-sacrifice. And fear not the momentary vacuum, the momentary aloneness. For God will fill your soul and body and mind with the very presence of a living flame.

I am your comforter as you seek to be that Comforter to all mankind.

Lanello

The Discipline of the Mind

Meditation/Concentration

for your Virgo initiation on the path of the Heart ♍

chapter nine

Moving toward the center
of a spiral nebula,
its flaming nucleus
in your heart,
you feel
the energies
of consciousness:

*... You contemplate Self
as a blazing sun.
You enter
the Crystalline Sphere
of the Holy of Holies.
You become
God
cycle by cycle.*

O Minds Upheld as Chalices of
  Living Flame!

   I am come to deliver unto you
wisdom's spiral—a spiral of the
Cosmic Christ consciousness that
originates in cloven tongues of the
Holy Spirit that are the love of God
for the wisdom of his law.

   As you have pursued the wings
of love, so I say, now perceive the
fires of Christ-mindedness and
become the presence of the Christ
mind.

   Now, my friends, if you will, as
you are meditating, see before you
a line horizontal just at eye level.
And for the graphics of contemplation,

imagine that all that falls beneath this line, as it were, of Christly demarcation is a perversion of the emotional and physical consciousness, and all that falls above it a perversion of the etheric and mental.

Most of you have an accurate sense of knowing when you are on the line of your Christly faculties and when you are off. Almost like a tightrope walker, mankind teeter and totter on this line of the Christ. And without the expertise that derives from the balance of the threefold flame, they often fall into the abyss of the illusions and perversions that come from the misuse of the four planes of Mater.

Some teachers have referred to the state of awareness or nonawareness in Christ as being "on the beam" or "off the beam." Again, the "beam" represents the fine line of Christ-discrimination whereon the consciousness of the soul, which we term *solar awareness,* merges and blends with the consciousness of the beloved Christ Self.

The Christ Self is the impersonal personality of the

Godhead descended from on high
to the point of the Mediator. And
that Mediator, when fully adored
by the soul, does become the Word
incarnate—the Word that is made
flesh and that dwells among
mankind, veiled in flesh yet still
"a light to lighten the Gentiles."[1]

When I think of maintaining
the Christ consciousness, I think of
children who like to balance by
walking on a curb or a line painted
on the street, children playing
hopscotch or striving for perfection
in games that test the poise of the
physical body, the marksmanship of
the eye as the arrow that is shot to
the center of the target, or the sheer
fun of trying to rub the tummy
and pat the head simultaneously as
emotional energies are brought
under control.

Thus the flowing stream of
consciousness willingly and lovingly
submits to the discipline of the will
that is a razor's edge of that mind
which has forsaken all for the goal
of oneness with the line of truth.

It is, then, to the discipline
of the mind that I would call your
attention. For some who would

meditate know not how to
meditate—that is, to draw their
energies into the central forcefield
of the heart, to draw in all thoughts
and the sense of outer wings and
things that scatter the energies of
the mind, as the undisciplined eye
follows each passing fly or moth or
butterfly or bird across the sky.

Ask yourself this question,
O chelas of Morya, would-be chelas
of the Holy Spirit—ask yourself this
question:

Are you able to control thought
as the tautness of the string of a
harp, a violin, or a cello? Are you
able to tune the mind to the chord
of the Christ, to the tone of Life?
Do you know when your thinking
is on pitch—neither sharp nor flat?

Have you known the joy of
maintaining thought at the crest of
the wave?

And during meditation, are you
able to contemplate the octagon
crystal that contains the flame of
white-fire light from which may be
drawn forth at will the aspects of
the seven rays of the Holy Spirit?

O children who have gone
forth from the bosom of Abraham,

children of Israel, I call to you
now—come home to the center of
the flame of Christ-awareness, to
the center of flaming crystal!

And as you read my words,
seated in a place of quiet, posture
erect out of respect for the Spirit,
a breathless awe of the law, and in
the fear of the Lord that is the
beginning of wisdom[2]—let me
sketch for you on the canvas of
your mind a thought form that is
for the discipline of your faculties
in meditation.

First let me explain that in
order for you to function properly
in the world of cause/effect in
Matter form, it is necessary that
your energies be extended through
the nervous system, through the
senses, and through the aura for the
penetration of time and space, for
a grasp of actualities here below,
and for the mastering of conditions
and circumstances. When your
energies are thus extended to fill
the aura of selfhood in form, you
are in a state of *outer* awareness and
outer consciousness.

When the masters talk about
"going within," they mean that the

energies which have been dispersed, so to speak, for outer probing must be withdrawn into the chamber of the heart as an infolding spiral—as a fire infolding itself.[3] And thus the term *going within,* when properly understood, means spiraling back to the fiery core of the heart, which you may visualize as the centripetal movement of wind or water into the eye or focus of Self-awareness.

As we begin our exercise in meditation, I am then, with your kind permission, sketching upon the screen of your mind minute particles of energy—thought energy, emotional energy, and even the energies of the physical and etheric bodies—moving vortexlike toward the center of what you may visualize as a spiral nebula superimposed upon your being with its flaming nucleus in your heart.

Now, if it is your pleasure, sit back for a moment in your chair, close your eyes, and feel the energies of consciousness moving from outer sensation and outer awareness into the central flame of Life which you now see as the threefold flame burning steadfastly on the altar of the heart.

The energy moves toward this central sun of your being in a counterclockwise direction according to your own perspective. Thus the curve would move, below the heart, from the right side to the left and into the center; and, above the heart, from the left side to the right. This movement occurs as you contemplate Self as a blazing sun becoming more and more concentrated within the heart.

Close your eyes and visualize the sun of the Christ consciousness as that dazzling white-yellow glory now the size of a beach ball encompassing your heart and chest cavity.

The more you contemplate this sun, the less you are aware of outer conditions until, unable to resist the magnet of God's love, wisdom, and power, you plunge into the center of this sun, magnetized by the Presence of Life and the calling of home which suddenly, through the mind's eye, has become so close, so warm, so sacred.

Now you perceive the wonder of celestial bodies, of the evening

star, of man's outer adoration
become the blazing glory of man's
inner realization.

Behold a celestial sphere
suspended in spacelessness around
the heart!

Behold the heart suspended in
the timelessness of the sphere!

Behold the entering in to the
Holy of Holies as man becomes
God cycle by cycle, year by year!

As you contemplate the
wonder of the spiral nebula of
being moving into the center of
our oneness, you penetrate the world
of crystalline dimensions. Of
chalcedony, agate, and chrysoprase.
Of kunzite, sphalerite, labradorite,
and alexandrite. Of ruby, sapphire,
diamond, emerald, and aquamarine.

Such are the geometric
crystallizations of the Christ mind
and of the soul that has begun
the mastery of Life all one—of Life as
Mother flow into the schemata of
the Elohim here below.

Now, inasmuch as the energies
of God coalesce in form according
to the patterns of crystal,[4] I urge
you to meditate upon all aspects of
crystal which the elementals have

defined in their role as instruments for the handiwork of the Mother.

Yes, I say, meditate upon crystal forms that are revealed by a microscope as well as to the naked eye. And in following these lines of force, your consciousness will always return to the point of origin—the point of the flame and the nexus of the source that is in the eye of the flame.

Likewise, it would be well in the training of the mind to peruse Saint Germain's *Studies in Alchemy*[5] and to outline for yourself thirty-three points of precipitation which are yours to discover in his timeless release on the laws of the transfer of energy from the plane of Spirit to the plane of Mater.

And next week I shall continue for you my sketch for meditation which you may call your own as you resist not my markings on the screen of your mind.

I AM forever marking the way of victory for all.

I AM Mark in the geometry of

Lanello

Chambers
of Consciousness

Purification/Penetration

for your Libra initiation on the path of the Heart ♎

chapter ten

From the center
of the globe
in the fiery lotus
of the heart,
you project
golden star-fire light ...

...bursting fiery snowballs
consume all anti-Love
and you create
the habitation of
the Most High God.

To You Who Remain Suspended
 in the Sphere of the Crystalline
 Consciousness of the Son,

    Have you tarried in the
bliss of God? Have the joys of the
inner penetration of the very
substance of the source of life
replaced your frolicking and fretting
in the outerness of mortals?
    I can well understand! For
whether you know it or not, you
have begun the exploration of the
diamond-shining mind of God.
    Right within your very being,
you have begun the journey
through infinity which joyfully, by
his grace, will never end. Indeed,

this is a most extraordinary method of disciplining the energies of thought, of desire, and of will.

Pour forth your love to God, O mortals, and be swallowed up in immortality!

Have you heard the soundless sound of the moving of love?

Have you perceived when love moves from the finite to the infinite?

Do you know when your grasp of a cosmic concept has allowed you to pass from the mind of man to the mind of God?

Do you perceive the spirals of your ascending consciousness?

I say, nay.

O children on the belt of time and space, you do not perceive the movement of being along the lines of force and the grids of consciousness that carry every pilgrim of peace from dimension to dimension as the miles of initiation move the bearer of faith, hope, and charity imperceptibly from the highways of this world to those of the next.

And the gentle shifting of consciousness from light to greater light, to the glory of other years and yods, is the easing of consciousness from plane to plane until the soul enters the great hall of a heavenly Versailles and the throne room of the Sun King, the Christ who rules as the personification of the law in the great three-in-one of Life.

Hearken, then, O children of the Sun King and the Sun Queen! Hearken, children of Helios and Vesta destined to be adorned with the robes of white-fire crystal, bright pink and gold, sealed in a sphere of blue of the Buddha's adoration of the Cosmic Virgin!

As you meditate upon the source of being, you cannot fail to give gratitude, profound and ever flowing, to the disc of light that adorns the sky, adoring a love beyond our ken yet within our all-knowing.

As you allow your energies and consciousness to flow in meditation upon the crystals of nature, and as the fingers of the mind fondle the tenets of the Master Alchemist— so you create channels whereby the light flows as on rays of sunlight to the concentration of the fiery core within the sun, that white-fire ball of piercing brilliance that now becomes the center of your meditation in the heart chakra.

Seated in the lotus posture or as you are most comfortable, now call upon the Christ to discipline all energy of life and being to be compressed in and as the nucleus of the atom of Self.

Realize that in consciousness you yourself must enter this nucleus just as though you were actually stepping into a translucent mother-of-pearl globe. Here you find a forcefield teeming with life and complexity yet compressed for a concentration of light that will be released at the conclusion of your ritual—for a controlled bursting out of energy according to the lines of flux predetermined by your own Christ consciousness.

Now you take your place on the throne in the center of the globe. This is the fiery lotus of the heart from which you command all energies previously misqualified through the actions and interactions of the four lower bodies.

Having withdrawn from the world of experience and sensation

in and through those bodies, you
now see with objectivity the world
of maya and miasma which you
have made and called your own.
This outer world in which you live
with such subjectivity is now seen
beyond the globe, through the
impersonal eye of the Christ,
as a set of wheels within wheels,
the vehicles of your soul for this
incarnation—this opportunity to
become the Word incarnate.

From this vantage point, you
see your four lower bodies as
chambers of consciousness.
You can even think of them as a
four-story house—the physical body
corresponding to the basement and
the foundation, the emotional body
relating to the family activities that
take place on the ground floor,
the mental body indicating study,
contemplation, and the activities of
the mind on the first story, and
the etheric body in the upper rooms
or the attic representing the
records of the past and the
blueprint for the future.

And one body blends into the
next as, story by story, the steps of
initiation over the spiral staircase

take you from the basement to the
skylight where the rays of the sun
reveal even another segment of the
shining pathway that leads back
to the center.

In reality, the chamber of the
heart is a circular stairway to
the stars fashioned out of the
threefold flame—the sacred fire that
translates the human consciousness
into the divine.

Standing on the stairs as
though examining the house where
the soul will abide for a time,
you see cobwebs in the corners of
the attic, collections of odds and
ends, photographs representing
snapshots (or snap judgments)—a
coup d'oeil of the outer or inner
personality of the members of the
household. You see the records of
family life in all of its happiness,
moments of grief and strife, and the
working out of ever-present karma.

Somewhat burdened by the
weight of all that has transpired
here, you say to yourself:
What this house needs is redecorating,
new life, objects of art and
paintings, a place for the children
to play—to be merry and gay!

The kitchen needs modernizing and
the anchoring of a flame where the
mother prepares her daily offering
of breakfast, lunch, and dinner for
the nourishment of the form and
the nourishment of the soul.

And so—room by room,
story by story—you see the outplay
of the compartments of consciousness.

This is your home. You can
make it what you will.

You can fill it with life,
greenery, flowers, religious shrines.
A library that bears witness to the
learning of angels, masters, and
men. And a hearth where the flame
burns perpetually in memory of the
Ancient of Days who rekindled by
his own threefold flame the
Life of a planet and its people.[1]

Basking in the light of the
threefold flame, you see how you
can make your four lower bodies
a living Shamballa—a shrine
to the Buddha and to the
Christ consciousness that is the line,
the horizontal line, of the mind's eye.

And as you measure, line upon
line, the attainments of the day,
recognize that you, in the
oneness of the flame, are the

transforming power, wisdom, and love of the home that is becoming your castle.

And then your four lower bodies (instead of being a burden of depression, a source of aggravation, a platform for temptation and the pilfering and squandering of the energies of the Holy Spirit) can be your retreat— your own focus of the wisdom of the Buddha, the love of the Holy Spirit, and the powerful willing of the Elohim, willing the soul to take dominion over all energy spirals and to be freeborn.

Now then, in your meditation, by the Christ mind you project to every corner of your house, to every nook and cranny—*light! light! light!* You fling light as a child throwing snowballs—up and down, to the right, to the left—into every level of your four lower bodies.

The bursting ball of snow, as golden star-fire light, illumines all: the virtues of angelic visitants standing guard, and the ghosts of doubt and fear lurking in the shadows of mortal creation. And in the burst of fire, much is consumed—

and more is revealed that will be consumed in another round of your meditation.

How easy it is to project light as a golden snowball of purity into patterns of self-indulgence, habits of defiance, and deadly stubbornness that stifles every intuition of the heart and the gentle proddings of the soul as well!

As you meditate, then, upon the sun center of being, receive now the impression of crystal water falling upon you as a rushing, teeming waterfall from the I AM Presence on high and then being directed, through all of the chakras, to every plane and dimension in the house of being.

The light that courses through your being is given direction by the discipline of the Christ mind to move unfailingly to the mark of that density which must be shattered once, shattered again, and then dissolved in the blinding purity of Almighty God himself.

O how the awesome Presence of the Holy One does enter the sun of being! For day by day, as you follow this exercise and

continue your invocations to the
violet flame as you have been
taught to do, you are creating a
dwelling place fit for the evolution
of the soul. Moreover, you are
creating even now the habitation of
the Most High God.

And one day you will perceive
that your temple has become the
temple of the Holy Spirit. And you
will bid him welcome and you
will say, "Hail, Maha Chohan!"
And you will not be ashamed to bid
the Lord enter. For your house will
be clean and shiny and tidy.
And the guest, sometimes unseen,
will not only be welcome but he
will be at home.

Won't you continue your
exercise of love-flow here below—
and then see, as crystal spheres of
golden light, the wisdom of God
penetrating within/without the
sun-field of consciousness you have
established around the heart?

Won't you now take to your
heart the invocations of
wisdom's flame—giving utterance to
the golden pink glow ray (see p. 266),
that Helios and Vesta might come
to you and magnify the Lord

by the action of that magnet that
is the heart of God?

I have come to you in this Pearl
of Wisdom, bearing my love as a
glowing ball of golden pink light,
establishing around each of my
friends a forcefield of the flowing
garment of the All-in-all.

I AM *Lanello*
Child of Innocence' Might

The Pearl
of Great Price

Visualization / Focalization

for your Scorpio initiation on the path of the Heart ♏

chapter eleven

*Visualize
a beautiful pearl
rising from your heart
to the heart of Christ —
a gift of your love
to the Flaming One ...*

*... From your I AM Presence
the Pearl of Great Price
is bestowed upon
your heart,
nucleus for the creation
of a causal body
to magnify the Lord.*

To All Who Would Be
   Victors in Consciousness
   Both in Heaven and on Earth,

   The white-fire light within the
heart is not intended to be the soul's
resting place forever and a day.
   It is a point of bliss to which
the soul may return for refreshment
and re-creation in a concentrated
focus of the sacred fire. It is a place
where the soul may tarry—where
the mind may contemplate God and
the heart may send love to the
Creator and the creation.
   Here is the forcefield where
every element of being is recharged
for a cosmic purpose—and a

cosmic fling! And so we come now
to the exercise for the controlled
bursting out of energy, of which I
spoke in my last release.

You may ask, What is this
controlled bursting out of energy?
And I will say, It is not a
volcanic eruption nor the wild fury
of a hurricane nor the sudden
movement of an avalanche of
ice and snow. Think of this
bursting out as the release of
Helios and Vesta—of energy from
the center of the sun of being
which, although it comes forth with
a tremendous imploding and
exploding of light, reaches the
farthest corners of the universe with
a gentle beam and a life-giving
radiance that signifies the flame of
mastery within and without.

And so, as your solar
awareness has tarried in the center
of the white-fire core of being in
meditation upon the law, in giving
forth invocations in the name of the
Christ and adorations of love for
the I AM Presence—all of this
energy, concentrated as a kernel
of being, as a seed of light, is
waiting to burst forth to adorn the

cosmos with the fruits of the sacred labor.

Now then, at the conclusion of your exercise in the white-fire core, call in the name of the Christ to the heart of the Father/Mother God to release with God-power, God-control, God-harmony, and God-reality the energies of your meditation into the etheric plane, the mental plane, the emotional plane, and the physical plane.

Call in the name of the Christ to the Great Divine Director, beloved Helios and Vesta, beloved God Harmony and Serapis Bey, and beloved mighty Victory to guard this bursting forth of energy and to retain it at first in the outer sphere (the beach ball) which you have coalesced around the heart and the chest cavity.

And so, from the nucleus of the atom, energy bursts forth to the first ring of awareness. And the particles of energy which moved toward the center of your spiral nebula—having been bathed, transmuted, and transformed in the sacred fires of the heart—move in an outward clockwise direction from the heart, once again to fill the four lower bodies with light and light's dimension according to the line of Christly demarcation.

Concentric rings, or forcefields, expand from the heart in ever widening circles. One by one, these circles of light are filled with the energies which you have concentrated by your meditation in the flame—until your being, your consciousness, and your entire aura are filled with a new radiance, a strength, a wisdom, and a will that make you transparent.

And your soul, like a gossamer veil, receives the impartations of the Godhead as it resumes its place in its evolution in time and space, penetrating outer consciousness with a new perception and a new poise of self-mastery.

You learn by this experience that energy is yours to command in the name of the Christ, that energy is God's gift to you, that energy comprises not only your form and your four lower bodies but also your consciousness and the forcefield of your world.

Each time you withdraw

into the inner Self and the inner chamber of the heart—first to purify, and then to concentrate this energy that it might become an acceptable offering unto God—there is a heavenly alchemy, a divine exchange, that occurs.

Let me explain.

When you enter into the Holy of Holies of the heart, exalting there the name of God I AM, there is a point in your meditation when this I AM THAT I AM (your own beloved individualized God Self) receives the holy offering of your purified energies as the nucleus of your consciousness.

When this occurs, the I AM Presence returns to you another nucleus, another forcefield of energy from on high—a sun molecule of light which is deposited in the forcefield of your heart chakra.

And thus the ritual of the alchemical marriage, whereby man offers himself up to God and God offers himself to man, is reenacted each time you properly complete your beach-ball exercise.

The energy which you give unto God is stored in your own

causal body as light's treasure in heaven. The energy which God gives to you is a gift of his momentum of concentrated fiery light that comes from the very center of the pulsating, flaming awareness that is the I AM Presence.

This, my beloved, is the putting on of the garment of the Lord.

On each successive occasion when you enter into meditation, you will have from your previous session a greater momentum of the Great Central Sun Magnet anchored within your heart for the drawing within of the particles of the four lower bodies. And this focus will in turn regenerate those particles so that your gift to the Almighty will also be a greater nucleus of light. When that offering is made at the conclusion of your exercise, the gift that is returned from the Presence is likewise proportionately greater.

You may visualize this flow—as above, so below—as a beautiful pearl rising from the heart of man, being received in the heart of the Christ, who in turn presents it on behalf of the soul to the Flaming One.

Simultaneously, there comes forth from the heart of this I AM Presence the pearl of great price that is delivered into the hand of the Christ Self, who bestows it upon the heart of the supplicant where it is retained by man as a magnet of His all-enfolding love.

Consider now how the pearl which comes down from the Father on high becomes the nucleus in the plane of Mater for the spiraling forth of energies even from the heart of unascended man and unascended woman.

This most precious focus is, then, for the creation in this plane of another causal body—one of purity, light, and love that is intended to fill all time and space with the glow of far-off worlds and to magnetize enough light here below so that the individual, the planet, and the solar system might one day return to the plane of Spirit in the ritual of the ascension in the light.

And thus, like the oyster, you are creating—layer upon layer—

a pearl within your heart that grows
and grows and grows as you
expand your sun center through
proper spiritual exercise. This
is how your causal body on high
is increased as you magnify the
Spirit of the Lord by the
Christ flame within your heart.

As the pearls of light are
exchanged between God and man,
the movement of forcefields of light
from the heart of man to the heart
of God creates a filigree like unto a
bridal veil. And this bridal veil—
the symbol of the purity of the
virgin consciousness of the soul
which knows only God, which gives
its energy only to God—begins the
weaving of the wedding garment
that is the adornment of the soul.

This forcefield, or *antahkarana*,
is the necessary grid of consciousness
upon which the Elohim and the
Cosmic Christ, together with the
Christ Self and the soul of each one,
build the rising pyramid of Life that
is the platform for the ascension.

The parable of the wedding
garment,[1] then, is clear. No matter
how much the Father/Mother God
may love a soul, unless the soul is

wearing the wedding garment at the conclusion of its opportunity for incarnation, the judgment of the Lawgiver must ring forth:

"Bind him hand and foot, and take him away, and cast him into outer darkness; there shall be weeping and gnashing of teeth."

Therefore, let all know that "many are called, but few are chosen." Thus the Word of the Lord is pronounced within the souls of all who read this Pearl.

In these days when you are striving to fulfill the purpose of an embodiment and of many embodiments, remember how the merchant who, "when he had found one pearl of great price, went and sold all that he had and bought it."[2]

So the light that comes down to you in such torrents and with such grace in this hour of the open door is the pearl of great price. The very essence of the sacred fire that forms layer upon layer around the nucleus of your heart—it is the pearl that is not only your gift to God but also a magnet of receptivity, drawing from on high the gifts of the Holy Spirit.

Realize that this light that descends as a shimmering shower is to be used for the infilling of the four lower bodies with the Lord's Spirit and for the filling of the concentric rings of time and space with a conscious awareness of infinity that you can hold (believe it or not!) here and now within the finite realm.

Realize that the many who are called are like children who come to splash in the foaming waters of the sea and to build their castles in the sand. These love the light of God and they have dreams of glory and noble ideals. But many of them are content to remain as children—to play with their Father's energy and to bask in the warmth of the summer sun. Yet they refuse to assume the responsibility for that energy and for the disciplining of mind, heart, and soul on the line of the Christ consciousness.

Without that discipline, without that determination to garner within the tabernacle of being the light of the Holy Spirit, no permanent progress can be made on the Path.

As I look over the students,

I see that there are those who have been entertained by the Pearls of Wisdom and by the dictations of the ascended masters for many a year. And they have thought mistakenly that acquaintance with the Word and with the teachers was somehow equivalent to individual attainment.

I would be a betrayer of your best interests and of your victory and your ascension, both here on earth and in heaven, if I did not warn you of the serious consequences of the continual misuse of God's energy.

This is especially of concern to the hierarchy as they consider what the students have done with the great dispensations of light that have come forth in recent classes.[3] For in order to give greater light and to place in hearts afire with disciplined love the energies necessary for the holding of the balance of the age, more among mankind—but especially more of the devotees—must offer the willing sacrifice of undisciplined lives, of scattered emotions and turgid mentalities, upon the altar of transmutation. These unbridled states of the ego must be redeemed for the fullness of the balance of Christ-power, Christ-wisdom, and Christ-love.

And so I say, begin this very day to cease the dissipation of your energies. Determine instead to discipline them along the lines of force outlined by your own Christ mind.

And one day, when you are called by the Christ and bidden to the marriage feast, you will come in wearing the wedding garment and you will be received as a candidate for the ascension at the retreat at Luxor.[4]

Perhaps then you will remember the communion we shared in these Pearls of Wisdom as we learned a little more about the putting on of the garment of the Lord.

I AM clothed upon this day with the glory of the One. Come ye into the union of the One.

I AM

Lanello

Flame of
His Very Flame

Communion/Cooperation

for your Sagittarius initiation on the path of the Heart ♐

chapter twelve

*Merge with the
masterful consciousness
of the Teacher,
take up the mantle
of the prophet
with dominion
over the elements...*

...eat His flesh
drink His blood
commune...in Love
assimilate...in Love
affirm...in Love
become
One
with every Keeper of the Flame..
in Love.

To You Who Are Waiting
  to Receive His Mantle and His Flame,

There comes a time in the life
of every disciple of the Christ when
he must be found ready to receive
not only the mantle of his master
but also the flame of his very flame.
When Elijah ascended into
heaven in a whirlwind,[1] he did so
with the certain knowledge that
his disciple Elisha would carry on
his mission in his mantle and
in his flame.
Elisha saw his master taken up
in the ritual of the ascension. And
he could perceive the wonder and
the glory of his reunion with God,

for he dwelt not in the consciousness of sackcloth and mourning. He "took hold of his own clothes and rent them in two pieces" as a symbol of the breaking of the limited cup of his consciousness and its exchange for the masterful consciousness of Elijah.

Thus, having shattered the modes of his former identity, he was able to take up the mantle of the prophet that fell from him. And immediately he smote the waters with the challenge "Where is the Lord God of Elijah?" In response to his command, the waters parted hither and thither and Elisha went over—showing his dominion in fire and water, air and earth.

In this episode there was imparted to Elisha not only the mantle, transferring the momentum of his teacher's consciousness of self-mastery, but there was bestowed upon him the unseen gift of the Holy Spirit, the flame of very flame—the very heartbeat of Elijah.

And so, Elisha partook of the body and the blood of the ascending one—the same Alpha and Omega

spirals that later, in another life,
the disciple now become the teacher
would impart to his own disciples,
saying: "Except ye eat the flesh of
the Son of man and drink his
blood, ye have no life in you.
Whoso eateth my flesh and
drinketh my blood hath eternal life,
and I will raise him up at the
last day."[2]

Are you ready, blessed ones, to
drink the blood of the hierarch and
to partake of his flesh? Do you
know the meaning of this
Sacred Communion wherein the
disciple assimilates the essence of
the sacred fire which is not only
symbolized by the blood but which
actually flows in the blood of the
Christed one?

Are you ready to be a
cell in the body of your Lord?
Do you sense that you are a part of
the body of the Mother?

Do you love enough to give
your body to the master?
Are you joyous when he is joyous?
Do you laugh when he laughs?
And do you feel the pain of the
world as he knows that pain?

Then you are coming closer

and closer to the flame.

Then you realize there is more
to this putting on of the
garment of the Lord than the
transfer of the mantle.

There is a merging with the
flame of being that must be
accomplished—and that can be
accomplished only as you love the
teacher even more than your life
and as you feel no separation but
a part of the whole of his
consciousness that has already
merged with the Whole
as the drop merges with the ocean.

Hence you claim no selfhood
apart from the teacher. And you
come to the inner meaning of the
calling of the disciple—and that is to
be disciplined to the place where
you become the living, breathing
awareness of the Presence of the
teacher.

In fact, then you are the
teacher.

And when this transition takes
place, you will know that you have
moved on the scale from the level
of disciple to the level of teacher.
And by so doing, you have
liberated the teacher for higher

service in the ascended master octaves.

As I mentioned to you earlier in the series, we desire to transfer to the devotees an increment of the flame of the Holy Spirit as we are merging our auras with your own.

We have shown you a number of methods as well as practical exercises for the putting on of the garment of the Lord, for the purifying of your energies in meditation, and for the offering up of the pearl of consciousness to the Presence, that you might receive in turn the pearl of great price from the heart of your Presence.

The rituals of the sphere and the fiery core within the sphere— and of the drawing within, in the great inbreath, particles of being for a concentrated bursting forth of energy—are intended to lead you nearer and nearer to the goal of receiving an increment of the flame of the Maha Chohan.

Some of you, because you have been preparing for many years for this initiation, will experience that transfer with the final release in this series. Others will take my Pearls and study them and pore over them until the quickening comes, as on the day of Pentecost.

Then the wind rushing through the tall pines or the palm trees will signal a presence that is more than that of sylphs. It will signal the presence of the Maha Chohan.

To be "all with one accord in one place,"[3] as the disciples were on the day of Pentecost, means to be found in harmony with the Christ in every one of the members of the body of God. It means to be found in the likeness of the geometry of the law of harmony.

It means to be transparent for the flow of fire.

The cloven tongues of fire that sat upon each of them are the twin flames of Alpha and Omega; and they signify that each one has partaken of the blood (Alpha) and the body (Omega) of the Christ.

These cloven tongues, as the wings of the Spirit which alighted upon Jesus like a dove when he went to be baptized of John in Jordan, are the seal of the love of the Father/Mother God bestowed on this "my beloved Son, in whom I AM well pleased."[4]

Being one with the Christ of every member of the body of God, the disciple who has received the flame of the Holy Spirit is able to speak with other tongues—not only the tongues of men, but also the tongues of angels—as the Spirit gives utterance to the affirmation of the Word in every facet of the jewel of the Christ consciousness as it is reflected in angels, elementals, masters, and the sea of humanity.

Paul said that to affirm that Jesus is the Lord can come only by the Holy Ghost.[5] Indeed, it is the Holy Spirit that reveals to every heart the true nature of man and woman to be the Christ. And without that Spirit you can neither see, nor feel, nor hear, nor touch, nor taste that Christ—whether in the teacher, in the Mother, or in yourself.

To each of the disciples is given a gift of the Spirit. This comes about as the Holy Spirit quickens within each one a specific aspect of the causal body. This is released by divine decree as a dispensation of light—a descending

pearl of great price, if you will—
which bursts in the consciousness
and illumines the mind.

And so Paul saw the diversities
of operations as being "the same
God which worketh all in all."[6]

And he preached to the early
Christians of the oneness of the
body of God and of all being
baptized into one body: "Whether
we be Jews or Gentiles, whether we
be bond or free, we have been all
made to drink into one Spirit."[7]
And thus there is no schism in the
body of the Lord, as the members
have the same care one for another
as they do for themselves.

And thus the gifts of the Spirit
become the flame that enhances the
sacred labor of each part of the
body as "to one is given by the
Spirit the word of wisdom;
to another the word of knowledge
by the same Spirit; to another faith
by the same Spirit; to another the gifts
of healing by the same Spirit;
to another the working of miracles;
to another prophecy; to another
discerning of spirits; to another
divers kinds of tongues; to another
the interpretation of tongues: but all

these worketh that one and the selfsame Spirit, dividing to every man severally as he will."[8]

This, then, is the communion of the Lord in this age. And this is his communication.

If you will merge with one another in love, in bearing one another's burdens and in exchanging those burdens for the light causal body of Jesus the Christ himself—then the Holy Spirit will come to you.

Do you understand that no one man, no one woman can contain the allness of that Spirit in the plane of Mater? Only in the ascended state can the fullness of that Spirit be realized in being and in individualized consciousness.

Here on earth, then, the ultimate requirement for the getting of the Holy Spirit is the joyous communion and the love-flow between the members of the body of Christ as Keepers of the Flame serve together with one accord (with one vibration) in one place (in one consciousness), daily merging their energies in the giving of the Ave Maria—the praise to the

Cosmic Virgin that arcs the worlds
with the resounding "Hail Mary,
full of grace. The Lord is with thee!"

As they serve together as the staff
upholding the office and the mission
of the messengers, as they serve one
by one in the fields that are white to
harvest,[9] laboring a labor of love for
the Lord—they are found one in
consciousness. Thus they are one at a
certain plane of the Christ mind
where they converge in the canopy of
the Lord's host hovering over an
infant humanity in the manner of the
covering cherubim who keep the
flame of the ark of the covenant.

And so as Keepers of the Flame
around the world merge the energies
of their daily devotions, their service,
and their selfless love, they are found
to be one on the line of the Christ
mind. And there on that line they find
the geometrization of the mind of God
to be the release of the afflatus of the
Holy Spirit.

Wait patiently upon the Lord, all
ye who would know him. For he will
surely come. He will surely come.[10]

Although you are separated by
the miles, by mountains and oceans
and a diversity of occupations—

remember that as you serve the one
God in demonstration of the law of
hierarchy, by that same law you must
be found one, not only with those
who are of like mind in this age but
with all others in all past ages who
have ever returned to the oneness of
the flame.

This oneness is the same
whirlwind into which Elijah ascended.
It is the movement of the consciousness
of souls striving at a certain tension,
a certain frequency and vibration.

And until that plane is reached,
you will not know what it means to
be a part of the entire Spirit of the
Great White Brotherhood
which functions as the arm of the
Holy Spirit at both unascended and
ascended levels.

There is always so much talk
about the amalgamation of new-age
groups and the coming together of
Christians and others in an ecumenical
spirit to the glory of God. This is
indeed a worthy goal.

But may I say that in all of my
experience upon earth, I have found
that the only true unity that has ever
come about has been the unity of the
Christ mind.

And therefore hierarchy allows the sheep to be scattered over the hillsides of the world until they come together through the door of the sheepfold because they know the voice of the Good Shepherd.[11] And the only way that that voice can be known is through the presence of the Holy Ghost.

Therefore, we instruct. We send forth our Pearls to the farthest reaches of the earth. And step by step, one by one, the disciples come into that Christ awareness which magnetizes the Spirit—and which in turn is increased by the Spirit that is magnetized—until those who are ready are brought into the levels of organization where cooperation in a spirit of harmony is the next step on the ladder of attainment.

Hierarchy is no longer willing to bring into organizations sponsored by the ascended masters those who are discordant or those who introduce spirals of disintegration through the rot and the decay of the untransmuted ego.

For the body of God must be integrated. And this means the meshing of gears from one disciple

to the next until the highest initiate
unascended meshes the gears of
consciousness with the ascended
hierarchy.

And so our organization upon
earth is a succession of wheels
moving with wheels and the hum of
a giant motor that is, so to speak,
a geometrized version of the
body of God.

But this is not the
mechanization concept. This
is the automatic integration of all
souls who are one in Christ by the
Lord's Spirit with the very fires of
creativity that are the essence of
God's being.

Now, precious souls, prepare
for our final releases which will be
complete with number fourteen in
this series. Prepare yourselves with
fervent devotion for this
oneness in the body of God by
rendering service unto the least and
the greatest among your fellow
servants in the Cause.

Commune in love. Move in love.
And let your conversations be in love.
And let us see if we can—for a
moment and then for a succession
of moments, moving into the hours

and days of the Lord's cycles—hold
the body of God at a certain pitch
of the Christ mind so that countless
numbers who read my words will
be prepared with one accord in one
place for the reception of the
Holy Ghost.

I AM with you always,
even as I AM everywhere in the
consciousness of God in manifestation
within you.

Lanello

Toss the Ball!

Magnetization / Impartation

for your Capricorn initiation on the path of the Heart ♑

chapter thirteen

*Whirling pearls
of sacred fire
going forth
from your heart
to souls yearning
for peace...*

*...spheres of
    cosmic consciousness
    burst aflame
    in children of the Sun
    —you must share
    in the cadence of our Love.
        I care.*

And So, My Beloved,

I come to you in the presence of a love that we have shared, not for one life but for many lives.

And our longing to be one— your longing to be one with me and my longing to hold you in the embrace of the ascended master consciousness—sets up a polarity between heaven and earth that is a magnet of love whereby your yearning to come home daily propels your consciousness higher and higher into the realm of Spirit even as you cast the net of your consciousness into the depths of the cosmic sea.

Desiring to be loved, to be free,
to be whole, is the legitimate
striving of the soul for union
with the I AM Presence. And each
successive entering in to that
Presence through sacred
communion and meditation
increases the desire for oneness,
even as the desire is fulfilled.

Like the sweetness of
honeysuckle on the summer breeze,
you drink in the flame. You are
surfeited with God's love.

You are satisfied for a moment.
But then, having tasted the bliss
of his consciousness, you desire
even more and then more.

And again you drink in the
fragrance of love. You are filled
and you think that your soul will
never be able to contain the love of
God until another day when,

By your desiring God,
You have become on earth
As in the flaming yod—
A galaxy of God
Desiring to be God.

As you increase the magnet of
the heart's love by loving God,
forming a sun of even pressure
around the heart—spinning

like a top, whirling by the motion
of his love—realize that having
created this sun center, you are now
in a position to create other
worlds of causation.

As the sun of the heart is
composed of energies gathering in a
focus of devotion and desiring
to be, so

It is a causal body here below
Whirling in time and space
That all might know
That God is as real on earth
As he is in heaven,
That to each one—
To each perfected daughter
    and son—
He has imparted the secret
    of the leaven.
And the leaven is the
    lump of gold,
Of fiery love from worlds untold
Concentrated as energy's pearl—
A causal body, a cosmic whirl
That Elohim and Christ Self
    now do hurl.

Whatever you create within the
heart of purity and perfection,
you can project to any point in
time and space.

By the action of cosmic grace

in and through the threefold
Christed flame, you can repeat the
electronic pattern of the heart,
the fiery ball, the mother-of-pearl,
by a thrusting of the mind and
consciousness, by a willing in
God's will to be that purity and that
perfection—anytime, anywhere.

For, you see, it is the
I AM Presence, through your
knowing and your seeing and your
proving of the law, that has brought
forth in you this masterpiece, this
sphere of iridescent light. And the
I AM Presence is capable of
projecting that sphere, that image of
the Christ, that forcefield of cosmic
consciousness, to any point in time
and space throughout the cosmic
egg or on the curve of infinity as it
pleases the I AM THAT I AM.

Take then, beloved ones, my
proffered gift—my love whereby
I place upon you now the garment
of my consciousness of love.

Let me help you with that
cloak. Won't you put your arms
into the sleeves as I assist you?

Won't you take the gift then
and understand that as you have
apprenticed yourselves to me,

an artisan of the Spirit, you have
learned to chisel out of light, to etch
in fire, and to coalesce molecules by
the power of the spoken Word—
to create (what else?) the perfect
sphere, the perfect pearl.

As you have created one, so
you can create many. The pattern
may be duplicated again and again.
You have then but to make the call
to the I AM Presence and to me
in the name of the Christ

To duplicate the offering of the
    causal body rare
Wherever hearts with a sigh
    in silent prayer
Do plead before the bar
    for freedom from bondage,
From sickness and from sin—
Wherever minds reach up for
    perfection's mark
And souls chant the hymn
    of the sacred ark.

The pearl of great price
    of your I AM Presence
Can be hurled to every soul in need—
'Twill reach the mark with victory
    and godspeed!
This is how the Lord answers
    the prayers of the humble
Offered unto the saints.

This is how the Lord distributes
   the manna of his love—
"Give us this day our daily bread,"
As sacred scriptures are being read
And the recitation and the response
   is being said.
This is how hierarchy,
   sponsoring the faithful
In all the churches, mosques, and
   temples of the world,
Reaches out from the center of God
To deliver the law and the divining
   of his rod.

Not one, not a million or a billion,
But an infinity of whirling
   pearls of sacred fire
Can go forth from your heart
   hour by hour
As your heart becomes the
   seat of authority
And your love the scepter of priority.

To will to love, to love to will—
This is the signet of the priest-kings.
And thus the rule, the golden rule,
Of new-age hierarchs
Who stand upon the mountains
   of the world—
Feet firmly planted on the earth,
Hearts meshing with Spirit's new birth—
Come forth to declare
The government by sacred law

And honor in the flame.
These are our emissaries come
    to rule in his name.

We are the sponsors of a new race
And a new course of civilization
    unbound.
Will you sponsor lifewaves
By enfolding life with a
    daily release
Of causal bodies round?
Will you inundate the earth
With spheres of violet, gold, and blue
Rolling down the hillsides,
Down the valleys through and through?
Like Omri-Tas,
    Ruler of the Violet Planet,
    and his priests,
Who sent forth one hundred
    and forty-four thousand
Violet-flame balls for the light
    and the victory
Of freedom's release.[1]
What cosmic beings have accomplished
You can, too,
By willing the light of the Christ
And keeping the flame anew!

Now see the pearl within your heart
Beginning to turn.
O see it whirl!
And as it whirls faster and faster,
Scintillating mother-of-pearl

Emitting crystal sparks
And starlike flashes—
Watch now how
Spheres of light
Of pink and green and white
Come forth from flaming spiral—
Threefold wonder of the heart!

Toss the ball, O children of the sun!
Toss the ball that hierarchy
   has tossed to you!
In this the game of life
   and the game of cosmos
No one is allowed to hold the ball.
Keep it moving, keep it moving,
   one and all!
Let none fall.
Let none miss the mark—
Let none miss in this game of life.

Throw that ball to souls
Waiting for a burst of illumination,
Yearning so for peace!
Toss the ball
And watch it burst aflame
In heart and mind and soul
Of one reaching up to catch the sphere
Of cosmic consciousness.

And so, my beloved,
With the yearning to be one,
To come home,
There is a yearning to share
All that you know,

All that you have been given,
With other parts of Love—
Other children of the sun.
So much love is compressed within
The fiery sphere of flaming sun
That you must share it
With another and another
    and another.

And so before you burst with love,
Quickly toss the ball
And see how with each tossing
    of the ball
The sphere multiplies
A thousand times a thousand
Until all of life
Is receiving and giving,
Receiving and giving,
Catching and throwing,
Throwing and catching
The endless chain of bubbles—
Bursting light bubbles
Of Christ Self-awareness,
Of godly good pleasure.
They are for the measure
Of the impartation
Of the cadence of love.
I AM for the One and the Whole
In the center of being of all.

Lanello

Call upon the Lord!

Glorification/Initiation

for your Cancer initiation on the path of the Heart ♋

chapter fourteen

I deliver to you
the scroll
of your initiation
in the trial by fire.
Praise God!
Affirm the eternality
of thy Being ...

... Surrender to God without qualification. Accept God without qualification. Call upon the Lord! Withhold nothing from Him and He will withhold nothing from thee.

To Those Who with Job
   Would Give Answer to the Lord,

   My God, "I know that thou
canst do every thing and that
no thought can be withholden
from thee.
   "Who is he that hideth counsel
without knowledge? Therefore have
I uttered what I understood not;
things too wonderful for me, which
I knew not. Hear, I beseech thee,
and I will speak: I will demand of
thee, and declare thou unto me.
   "I have heard of thee by the
hearing of the ear: but now mine
eye seeth thee."[1]
   The words of Job spoken unto

the Lord after his initiation of the trial by fire are a glorying of the Lord who made heaven and earth and of the law which keeps the stars in their courses and reveals the wonders of the atom.

Hearken unto me, children of the sun! Hearken unto me as I come to deliver to you the scroll of your initiation in the trial by fire! For the angels of record serving with the Keeper of the Scrolls have prepared for you a very personal initiation in the same fires which tried the faith, the hope, the will, and the humility of Job.

As you read the Book of Job and consider his trials and his testings—at times by his own karma, by the returning cycles of his own past uses and misuses of the law, and at times through direct confrontation with the adversary— consider what you would do if the law and the Lord required you to submit to those same trials and testings.

Would you respond as Job and return victoriously to the center of oneness? Or in your vanity, your immaturity, and your lack of vision,

would you respond as Eliphaz the
Temanite and Bildad the Shuhite
and Zophar the Naamathite?[2]
These three who compromised the
law of the Lord represent the failure
of the three lower bodies of
mankind to conform to the
harmony of the law through trust,
obedience, and love.

Entering into the higher planes
of the etheric consciousness,
centered in the soul that knows the
Christ, Job was the victor of the
divine blueprint and of the
law of Life for all who would follow
the Christ of the ages in the
regeneration of the sons of man,
that they might become the
Sons of God.

The Lord would never have
allowed the testing of Job if he did
not know that Job was equal to the
testing.

Therefore as your Christ Self,
the hallowed Mediator in the
fiery Logos, unwinds the scroll of
initiation—consider that for each
reader of the Pearls of Wisdom and
for each one who shall read these
words throughout all time and
space, there is prepared an initiation

specifically for your level of consciousness and for the level of your preparation.

We take into consideration your will and your willingness to align that will with the will of God. We watch the cycles of the unfoldment of karma—of energy spirals of past, present, and future.

We consider the factor of the adversary or perhaps the initiator in the Saturnian energies[3] and their cycling through the house of the Mother and of the Church Universal and Triumphant. We consider him to whom "it was given to make war with the saints and to overcome them." And we consider the power that "was given him over all kindreds and tongues and nations."[4]

We consider him to whom the Lord said, "Hast thou considered my servant Job, that there is none like him in the earth, a perfect and an upright man, one that feareth God and escheweth evil?"[5]

We behold the corona of the saints, of the Christed ones, and of the Keepers of the Flame who are sealed in a dimension of light's intention to be invincible, incorruptible in the face of the beast that ascendeth out of the bottomless pit.[6]

All initiations are intended to lead the soul and the evolving consciousness to the place where, drawing the sword of truth from the sheath of the will of God, man and woman slay the dragon of their own carnal-mindedness and put down the tempter who tempts the children of the dawn to curse God to his face.[7]

In the hour of the testing, see that you release praise for all of the good that has come forth from the hand of God. And fear not to praise him in the hour of temptation—in the hour when the last vestiges of the self must be sacrificed. And let the sealing of the lips be the mark of the attainment of Job.[8]

And when your "friends" come to mourn with you seven days and seven nights, grieving in the grief of mortality confined to mortality,[9] fear not to consign to the flame even the temptation to curse the day of your birth.[10]

Know then that your birth is

and was from the beginning the originating by the Father/Mother God of a unique idea to be sent forth upon the arrow of their love into this plane of limited self-awareness that you might gain, through the testing and the trial, an unlimited perception of idea as selfhood.

Finally, do not attempt to cancel out the initiation of the spiral of your being by Almighty God to compensate for the loss of outer identity that comes in the hour of the attainment of the inner *Id-Entity.*

O mortal, when thy soul is weighed in the balances, long not for death.[11] Run not from the Judge and the Lawgiver but stand before the judgment seat in the great throne room and affirm forever the eternality of thy being.

Fear not the avenging one. For he shall exact from thee only that which the Lord doth allow. And he shall take from thee only those things which thou hast failed to ratify as permanent modes of consciousness—as ideas fired in the kiln of Horeb's height.[12]

Are your possessions objects of the Spirit—objectifications of the

inner light of your attainment?
Or are your possessions the
acquisitions of the acquisitiveness of
vain selfhood? That which is of the
light shall be preserved of the light.
That which remaineth in outer
darkness shall be consumed.

Stand not in fear of the scourge
of God. And when the fires of
judgment come, say not, "The thing
which I greatly feared is come upon
me, and that which I was afraid of
is come unto me."[13]

For you to whom it is given to
have love and to have a measure of
the law which has not been given to
the earth for generations, there is no
need to tremble at the sacrifice
when the payment of the last
farthing is exacted.[14] When every jot
and tittle of the law is fulfilled, then
the balance of the scales of Libra
will find you in perfect equilibrium
on the line of the Christ consciousness.

As the postman delivers this
my final release, know then that the
angel of record places in your hand
the scroll on which there is
marked—as surely as the lines of
your hand—the path of attainment
for the balance of your life.

It is a chart, a road map, an outline. And your Christ Self will tutor you in the weeks and months ahead to show you how each measure of wheat, each measure of barley must be balanced—each erg of energy misqualified replaced with light and then balanced in the scales for the alignment of heart and mind, soul and memory as the four lower bodies are measured and weighed for the hour of the ascension.

Receive now, sons and daughters of Morya—receive now the eternal flame of the Maha Chohan. Accept the influx of the greater fire merging with the lesser fire of your being.

See now how the momentum, the fiery momentum of the Maha Chohan can merge with your own to increase the power, wisdom, and love of your own threefold flame, that you might also increase that fire here below with the golden glow of pink and blue and violet hue—sacred essence of the God I know.

O flaming hearts of Saint Germain, do you understand

the two factors essential to your reception of the flame? The first is unqualified surrender. The second is unqualified acceptance.

To be fearless in the divesting of oneself of the trappings of mortality, to be fearless in commanding the flame of God to leap within your heart, to enter there, and to impart the bestowal of the Holy Spirit—to accept without fear, without self-condemnation this gift of God: herein is the key to Aaron's rod.

Herein lies the scepter of authority.
Herein lies your dominion
   in the planes of Mater
To stand upon the rock of Christ
And to challenge without reserve
All aspects of the lesser self.
And then, having surrendered
   and having heard
The voice of God speaking the
   sacred Word
And from the summit of being
   the command
"Behold, I AM THAT I AM!"
You then are fearless to demand
The fullness of being here and now,
The long lost perfection of your
   holy vow.

Precious ones, it is guilt and guilt alone that comes from fearing the judgment of the law when you have forsaken the oneness of the flame that weighs you down and prevents your acceptance of the flame of the Maha Chohan.

Guilt is dark and dank. It is the basis of the feeling of unworthiness that stands between you and your God.

Do not allow the Liar to spawn the virus that consumes body and soul in this incubator of fear and guilt and worthlessness and separation from the Source that is the breeding ground for every form of disease known in the body of the earth.

Let the flame of the Christ consume the darkness and the dankness and be the light and the warmth of a healthy body, a healthy mind, a healthy soul. Let it consume the microbes of insanity and the trauma of nervous tension.

For it is my intention that you shall achieve in this dimension of time and space a strong heart, a sound mind, and an able body capable of fulfilling the mandates of the Lord. Therefore, call unto the

Lord in that holy innocence that
you once knew before your soul
descended from the heart of the
Presence and from the cycles of the
causal body.

Call upon the Lord
In holy innocence, in truth,
And in the cosmic honor flame.

Withhold nothing from him
And he will withhold nothing
   from thee.
This, my beloved, is the sacred key
Of the bestowal, of the mantle,
   of the flame—
In essence, of the putting on
Of the garment of the Lord.

And so I say it again:
Call upon the Lord!
Withhold nothing from him
And he will withhold nothing
   from thee.

Faithfully, I AM yours to command.
As the genie of the flame,
I come forth when you call my name.
And now I return
To the flame whence I came.

Lanello

*Receive now
the eternal flame
of the
Maha Chohan.*

I AM the Bridge
for the translation
of your soul...

*...from the planes
of Matter
to the planes
of Spirit.*

The Bridge

I stood on the bridge at midnight,
  As the clocks were striking the hour,
And the moon rose o'er the city,
  Behind the dark church-tower.

I saw her bright reflection
  In the waters under me,
Like a golden goblet falling
  And sinking into the sea.

And far in the hazy distance
  Of that lovely night in June,
The blaze of the flaming furnace
  Gleamed redder than the moon.

Among the long, black rafters
  The wavering shadows lay,
And the current that came from the ocean
  Seemed to lift and bear them away;

As, sweeping and eddying through them,
  Rose the belated tide,
And, streaming into the moonlight,
  The sea-weed floated wide.

And like those waters rushing
  Among the wooden piers,
A flood of thoughts came o'er me
  That filled my eyes with tears.

How often, O, how often,
  In the days that had gone by,
I had stood on that bridge at midnight
  And gazed on that wave and sky!

How often, O, how often,
  I had wished that the ebbing tide
Would bear me away on its bosom
  O'er the ocean wild and wide!

For my heart was hot and restless,
  And my life was full of care,
And the burden laid upon me
  Seemed greater than I could bear.

But now it has fallen from me,
  It is buried in the sea;
And only the sorrow of others
  Throws its shadow over me.

Yet whenever I cross the river
   On its bridge with wooden piers,
Like the odour of brine from the ocean
   Comes the thought of other years.

And I think how many thousands
   Of care-encumbered men,
Each bearing his burden of sorrow,
   Have crossed the bridge since then.

I see the long procession
   Still passing to and fro,
The young heart hot and restless,
   And the old subdued and slow!

And for ever and for ever,
   As long as the river flows,
As long as the heart has passions,
   As long as life has woes;

The moon and its broken reflection
   And its shadows shall appear,
As the symbol of love in heaven,
   And its wavering image here.

HENRY WADSWORTH LONGFELLOW

Lanello,
a Messenger
of God...

Beloved Sons and Daughters of God,

I greet you in the name of the
I AM THAT I AM and in the name
of my beloved whose soul
has only yesterday reunited with
the Spirit of Living Love.

Lanello was and is to all who
will hear him a messenger of God,
sponsored by the Great White
Brotherhood to set forth the
teachings of the ascended masters
for the Aquarian age.

To me he will always be my
twin flame, the voice of the Guru,
beloved consort and wise counselor
on the path of initiation. And
we are one in the cosmic cycles—from
the beginning of Alpha unto the
ending of Omega.

I met Lanello when he was
Mark L. Prophet on April 22, 1961,
in Boston, Massachusetts.
He was the mouthpiece of the Lord
and of the Lord's emissary,
Archangel Michael.

As I entered the sanctuary
where he had been sent by the
Brotherhood to deliver the message
of the great Prince of the Archangels,
I remembered the words of the
prophet Malachi. They were
suspended in my mind like crystal:

"Behold, I will send my
messenger, and he shall prepare the
way before me: and the Lord, whom
ye seek, shall suddenly come to his
temple, even the messenger of the
covenant, whom ye delight in:
behold, he shall come, saith the
Lord of hosts."

Taking my place with the
devotees who had assembled for
this auspicious meeting of heaven
and earth in the power of the
spoken Word, I saw him. The
Messenger. He was seated in a most
peaceful, powerful meditation
upon the Lord God.

I closed my eyes and my soul
moved with his into the Great Silence

"The Joy of God
in the flame of Mother
is the delight of my soul
and my reason for being.
For in Her Heart
the works of our hands
bear fruit and multiply,
and the sons of the Father
bring Her children Home.
May it be so, O Lord,
of thy servant Mark."

of the ascended masters' consciousness.
I was caught up in the mantle of the
prophet. And, by the momentum
of his cosmic consciousness,
I entered the Holy of Holies.

Time and space were not. It
was as if we had never left eternity.

Suspended in the great stillness
of the sea of light, we were
surveyors of the vast beauty of
hallowed space—girded tier upon
tier by angelic hosts, Elohim, and
hierarchies of the Central Sun.

I beheld worlds beyond worlds
teeming with intelligences who
formed the universal chain of being.

I saw myself and my beloved,
together with all sons and daughters
of God, as extensions of the
One Great Self—as individual links
in the cosmic chain of Life traversing
the planes of Spirit/Mater "going out
and coming in" to the octaves of
heaven and earth.

These spheres of Life, Light,
and Love—quivering with energy,
bathed in the golden-pink radiance
of Mind—are the habitation of
God-free beings. Some who, by free
will, have descended to terrestrial
existences, mastered the laws of

selfhood in time and space, and ascended to the Source whence they came. And others who have chosen to remain in Paradise, their celestial brightness never having been sullied by the sense of sin and struggle.

In a moment, in God, the drama of Light evolving light had unfolded before me. My soul knew Reality.

I saw the work that lay ahead: to transfer all of this—this joy, this soul memory of inner spheres— to the evolutions of earth who had forgotten their early descent and the way of the ascent. Alas, to rescue the lifewaves who had exchanged this Reality for a vast unreality that could only lead to the void of non-being.

I would be made ready.

We returned gently to the circle of light-bearers gathered around the one devoted to his calling—the witness of the Word.

I opened my eyes and I beheld the eyes of the one seated before me at the altar. My search for the Guru was ended. For I beheld not the eyes of man, but the eyes of God resting upon me through this most blessed manifestation of Himself.

All my life I had been

searching for those eyes and always before I had been disappointed. But on that day in April as the sun moved into the sign of Taurus, I saw the Eye behind the eyes and I made contact with the Great White Brotherhood. With Saint Germain, Master of the Aquarian Age, whose calling had been upon me since my nineteenth summer. And the Ascended Master El Morya, the Guru behind the guru. With Jesus Christ, the Saviour of my childhood. And Gautama Buddha, whose peace and presence had smiled upon my soul from birth.

And the Virgin Mary took my hand and placed it in the hand of the messenger and said, "Be thou made whole!" Archangel Michael delivered his memorable dictation setting free the people of Boston. And my mission with the emissaries of the Lord, the ascended masters, began.

These sons and daughters of God come in the Person of the Comforter, saying with Jesus, "Be of good cheer; I have overcome the world." Yet they remain His servants, our elder brothers and sisters dwelling with us and among us, though "just beyond the veils" of time and space.

One with the cycles of Eternity, they are nevertheless the very personal Presence of the Spirit of the Lord which has rested upon the prophets of Israel, the gurus of the Himalayas, and the flaming ones of every continent.

This book is by and about Lanello, the ascended master who was with us in the person of our beloved Messenger Mark L. Prophet and is today our Ever-Present Guru.

Mark was born on December 24, 1918, in Chippewa Falls, Wisconsin, the only son of Thomas and Mabel Prophet, and he ascended on February 26, 1973, from Colorado Springs, Colorado. I knew him for twelve years—first as chela of the will of God under the disciplines of El Morya, and then as honored wife and mother of our four children.

It was while I was a student at Boston University that El Morya called me to go to Washington to be trained by him to be the messenger for the Great White Brotherhood. His purpose was to prepare me for the transfer of the mantle of the prophet and the initiation of the "double portion" of the Lord's Spirit.

I learned that it is the function of the messenger, or prophet, to transfer spirals of cosmic consciousness and energy from the ascended masters to unascended souls.

In other words, to be the conductor of currents of the Light and Consciousness of the Logos from the planes of Spirit to the planes of Matter—from the point of Origin, or Cause, in the white-fire core of universal Being to the point of effect in the time/space world of individual manifestation.

I saw that the messenger stands at the nexus of the figure eight in the flow of light from God to man to deliver that light to the people as "the Word of the Lord" in the same manner in which it came to the prophets of old.

I understood that it is through this dispensation of the prophets that God has provided for the awakening and the quickening of earthbound souls to their heavenly estate. Thus the prophet is the

link between the world of the
Real and the unreal.

Shortly after my arrival in the
nation's capital, Mark told me that
as soon as the matrices and
frequencies of my consciousness
were aligned with El Morya,
Saint Germain would anoint me
and seal within my chakras and the
layers of the auric envelope
the geometric formulae, fohatic keys,
hieroglyphs, and ciphers necessary
for the messengership.

Mark added that after a
number of years, when I was ready,
he would transfer the garment of
the Lord's consciousness which he
wore as the authority of the
Great White Brotherhood. And then
he would take his leave of this octave
and hold the balance for the mission of
our two witnesses as a servant of God
in heaven, an ascended master.

My beloved stayed and taught me
day by day out of the depths of his
soul's communion with the Lord's hosts.

He gave to me the wisdom of
his heart, cherished from the
centuries, and the disciplines of the
Law—enigmatic, engrammic—without
which no chela can survive on the

path of initiation. He gave himself
to me both in the chastisements
of Love and in the true compassion
of the All Loving One. He gave himself
to me as the father of our children
and as the lover of my soul.

After I received Saint Germain's
anointing, the true blessing of the
prophet Samuel and the flame of
the World Mother, Mark and I
served side by side for ten years.

Now and then he would
remind me of the inevitable 'parting
for a season'. But though my soul
knew the hour and the day and
my heart was already pierced by the
sword of truth that he brought,
my mind sealed itself from the
inevitable reality.

But then it came. That
memorable day when the garment
of the Lord fell upon me. And
I stood by—helpless, heartbroken,
wanting utterly to die for him,
wanting ultimately to live for the
children, all of God's children—and
watched for forty-eight hours as I
saw his soul leave the body temple
and reunite with Christ in God in
the glory of the ascension.

Truly it was a moment of the

greatest sorrow and the greatest joy
that the boundaries of human
experience can afford. Yet even
then he never took his soul's
compassionate eyes from me,
upholding me as I would uphold him.

In a final gesture, he raised his
hand and blessed me—the parting
sign of Love and the promise
"It is but for a little while."

In my anguish I cried out to
the living God, "Why, O God!
Why must it be!" And inexorably,
compassionately, He answered me
in the words of Paul: "For this
corruptible *must* put on incorruption,
and this mortal *must* put on immortality."

Then I knew that his sudden
transition was in fulfillment of the
Law of Transcendence which Mark
himself had taught me: As God is
forever transcending Himself, so his
Son must also transcend the limits
of his self-expression.

That God whom Mark had
realized as himself—that Jesus Christ
who was his personal Saviour—
could no longer be expressed in
finite form. The Light of his soul
had exceeded the capacity of the
lower vehicle. He must put on the

higher. He *must* put on the formless form of the Infinite. He *must* put on the garment of the Lord. He must wear his God consciousness in heaven, that I might wear mine on earth.

Then I knew that for the servant of God, death is not cessation: it is translation. It is the law of life becoming Life.

Then Jesus took me to his heart and repeated the words of comfort he had given to his own:

"The hour is come, that the Son of man [the Christ, the Light, in man] should be glorified. Verily, verily, I say unto you, Except a corn of wheat fall into the ground and die, it abideth alone: but if it die, it bringeth forth much fruit.

"He that loveth his life shall lose it; and he that hateth his life in this world shall keep it unto life eternal. If any man serve me, let him follow me; and where I am, there shall also my servant be: if any man serve me, him will my Father honour."

Mark exchanged the body terrestrial for the body celestial that we might live to enter the

Holy of Holies as he did. The corn
of wheat would bring forth much
fruit in the hearts and souls of
thousands and one day millions
who would take up the mantle (the
momentum) of the prophet and go
forth to smite the waters of
Jordan—to cleave asunder the
Real from the unreal in the mass
consciousness, taking dominion over
fire, air, water, and earth "not by
might, nor by power, but by my
Spirit, saith the Lord of hosts."

Mark the servant and follower
of Jesus Christ was glorified with
the Son. In the ritual of the
ascension into the I AM THAT I AM—
the consummate glory of the
earthly life become the heavenly—
he was honored of "my Father."
Having hated (sacrificed) his life in
this world, the one for the many,
he would "keep it unto life eternal."

There followed the ritual of the
dissolution of the human ego and
its displacement by the Divine Ego
in the initiation of the transfiguration.
The Light Body of the ascended Guru
was made congruent with the soul
of the unascended chela. The cosmic
interchange was complete. In the

sacred fire of our hearts' union in Spirit and in Matter, Pisces became Aquarius.

This, my beloved, is the alchemy of the Guru/chela relationship that awaits you on the path of your soul's initiation under the ascended masters.

Now, almost five years have passed since I looked into the eyes of my ascending Beloved and vowed to finish the work he had begun. In reality he has not gone anywhere, but only changed the form of our Oneness. And so we are one in the fire and the zeal of mission with every light-bearer on earth and in heaven. And with the legions of the Lord's hosts, we "keep on keeping on."

Mark once said, "Ours must be a message of infinite love and we must demonstrate that love to the world."

This book is Lanello's message of infinite love dictated to me the year after his ascension. It is both his message and his demonstration of that love. It is his witness of the flame which he first adored and then became.

It is the deepest desire of Lanello's heart to teach God's children

how they, through the attainment
of cosmic consciousness, may put on
the garment of the Lord as he did—
both in this life and in the next.

His message is a practical
teaching, step by step in the
disciplines of wholeness and in the
meditation of the great sphere of
being that is God. His message is
the distillation of his soul's
experience in God during countless
incarnations on Earth, on Venus, on
Mercury, and in other systems of
worlds as God has formed and
reformed within him the fullness of
his own Self-awareness.

You may be interested to
know, as I was, just when the story
of Lanello began.

Aeons ago, bodhisattva
Sanat Kumara, whom the prophet
Daniel beheld as the Ancient of Days,
came from Venus to keep the flame
of Life on behalf of Earth's
evolutions. Many sons and
daughters of God volunteered to
accompany this emissary of the
Most High to rescue the children
of God from the darkness and
deception of the fallen ones who
had departed from the Lord through

disobedience to the Law of the One.

Lanello and I and many of you were with them.

It is our memory of that journey with Sanat Kumara which we would bring to you, beloved sons and daughters of God who were a part of the vow and the vision of that company. And we would tell the story to all who have heard the message of our brothers and sisters who have since ascended from our midst after delivering God's Word in the civilizations of East and West.

Lanello is a kindred soul, one whom I am certain you already know so well as fellow pilgrim on the trek of the millenniums.

He will tell you that he is "seized with a passion that is the love of God" and that his one great desire is to share with you and me his cup of cosmic consciousness which God has filled with joy.

Now see—his joy runneth over forming streams and rivulets flowing to our own hearts! The thread of his soul's evolution toward this supreme realization of being is revealed in his utterly pure

and simple sense of mission, which
is the single outstanding quality of
his many incarnations on earth in
which he has truly put on, lifetime
by lifetime, the garment of the Lord.

Lanello's incarnations are
noteworthy because they reveal the
unbroken thread of contact which
he maintained with the hierarchy of
God and which he used to weave
that seamless garment of being
self-realized as the I AM THAT I AM.
Through his incarnations (only a
few of which I am permitted to
reveal), we learn the lesson of our
own emerging Christhood.

We see him altogether human
like ourselves, all the while fulfilling
the Divine Potential. Here is no
glazed ceramic figurine dusty upon
the shelf, but the figure of a man
with the dust of the road and the
sweat of life's labor upon him, gladly.

He wins, not because he is
always right, right, right like the
mechanized robots of our religions
of idolatry. He wins because he is
Real. Because he endures his
imperfections until he is formed
and reformed in Christ.

Looking through the windows

of his soul and its continuous devotion to the divine design, we learn the lesson that he would teach us—that we too, because we are both human and divine, "can make our lives sublime and departing leave behind us footprints on the sands of time."

I knew Lanello on Atlantis as a priest in the Temple of the Logos where he served, a master of the science of invocation. I knew him as Lot when he pleaded with the Lord for the saving of Sodom and Gomorrah. And as the Pharaoh Ikhnaton thirty-three hundred years ago when we worshiped the sun as the symbol of the One, Aton—*at-one* with the Son of Love.

He was Aesop, martyred for his light that has lived on in his fabulous fables. I knew him as Mark the Evangelist, who wrote the account of the works of our Lord Jesus Christ as these were confided to him by Peter the Apostle.

Yes, I knew the soul of Origen of Alexandria, who dared to set forth the teachings of Jesus Christ on reincarnation and the heavenly hierarchy before the early dogmatists of the Church who destroyed all but fragments of his work—and would do so today, if they could.

And I knew him as Launcelot du Lac, knight champion of Camelot and the very heartbeat and soul of both Arthur and Guenevere. I was with him when as Clovis he united the people of France under the religion of Christ and the fleur-de-lis of Saint Germain.

I knew him when to the people of Islam he was Saladin, conqueror and unifier of the entire Mohammedan world. And again I looked into his eyes when as Bonaventure, the child healed by Saint Francis, he became Seraphic Doctor of the Church.

I think of him, too, as the soul of Hiawatha, legendary chief of the Iroquois nation, prophet of his people who departed "in the glory of the sunset, in the purple mist of evening."

I remember him as Louis XIV, the "Sun King," who sought to outpicture his soul's memory of the culture of Venus at the Court of Versailles. And I knew him as Longfellow, whose poetry captured the spirit and heart of America in the abiding flame of his Guru, El Morya.

Born in Russia at the turn of the century, had Lanello survived the Bolshevik Revolution, he was destined to unite the children of Mother Russia for a century of enlightened self-rule and the fullest development of the God-potential within and without. His message is for today—for the people of Russia as well as the United States, that they and every nation might achieve that soul liberation which the seed of the wicked have sought again and again to counteract.

But this they shall not do. Because it is not ordained of God. Because the flame of freedom burns on in the hearts and souls of millions who yesterday died for the state and today live again to swear allegiance to Almighty God and "eternal hostility over every form of tyranny over the mind of man."

Mark L. Prophet, twentieth-century master, interpreter of the mysteries which the Lord has "kept hidden from the foundation of the world," was all of these yet none of these. He was uniquely Mark and much more. He was and is a flame—active, vital, eternal!

He stands today a pillar of fire in the very midst of the people Israel—the prophet of the twelve tribes and of the thirteenth whose souls have reincarnated in America and in every nation on earth, among every race and people. Today as yesterday, he is speaking the prophecy for the return of the sons and daughters of God to the house of the Lord. He is setting forth the teachings of the science of the spoken Word and giving to us the initiations necessary for our soul's liberation in the ritual and the reunion of the ascension.

It was in the hour of his transition from time and space into the cycles of Eternity that he proclaimed, "Behold, I AM everywhere in the consciousness of God!"

John the Revelator wrote of the mission of our twin flames as Jesus Christ revealed it to him in the tenth and eleventh chapters of the Book of Revelation. "But in the days of the voice of the seventh angel, when he shall begin to sound. . ."

This is a veiled reference to the cycle of the Aquarian age—the seventh dispensation when Saint Germain, Lord of the Seventh Ray, comes to finish the revelation of "the mystery of God" begun by the Ancient of Days, which he declares "to his servants, the prophets." This they set forth in the "little book"—sweet in the mouth and bitter in the belly.

Empowered by God with the spirit of prophecy, it is the mission of the "two witnesses" to deliver to the souls of the "hundred forty and four thousand" as well as to every nation and kindred and tongue and people the "new song" and the "everlasting gospel" whereby they shall overcome the dragon "by the blood of the Lamb, and by the word of their testimony." Thus the teachings that are given forth in this book are the continuing testimony of our messengership before "the God of the Earth," Gautama Buddha. Sealed by the prophet Daniel, the mission marks the "time of trouble" when Archangel Michael should deliver the people found written in the Book of Life.

It was Daniel who looked and beheld the prophecy that I have lived through painfully, joyously—

"Behold, there stood other two, the one on this side of the bank of the river, and the other on that side of the bank of the river. . . .

"And one said to the man clothed in linen, which was upon the waters of the river, How long shall it be to the end of these wonders? And I heard the man clothed in linen, which was upon the waters of the river, when he held up his right hand and his left hand unto heaven, and sware by him that liveth for ever that it shall be for a time, times, and an half; and when he shall have accomplished to scatter the power of the holy people, all these things shall be finished."

The man clothed in linen is our Lord Jesus Christ, the Great Mediator of the Word and of the mission of the two witnesses. The scattering of the power of the holy people is the spreading abroad of the teachings of the ascended masters across the face of the whole earth, heart-flame to heart-flame, until

that power—the Christ consciousness—
is sealed in every child of God.

"And many of them that sleep
in the dust of the earth shall awake,
some to everlasting life, and some
to shame and everlasting contempt.
And they that be wise shall shine as
the brightness of the firmament;
and they that turn many to
righteousness as the stars for ever
and ever. . . . Many shall be
purified, and made white, and tried;
but the wicked shall do wickedly:
and none of the wicked shall
understand; but the wise shall
understand."

Today the ascended master
Lanello is the prophet who stands
with the Son of God in the octaves
of Spirit, prophesying and
preaching to the children of God on
earth. While, by the grace of God, I
am on this side of the bank of the
river in the planes of Matter,
receiving day by day the garment of
the Lord's consciousness and
putting it on His children.

If they would but accept it, all
twin flames have the selfsame
responsibility within their own
sphere of God Self-awareness to

fulfill the calling of the two witnesses and the other two. As Jesus spoke not alone for himself but for every son of God: "To this end was I born, and for this cause came I into the world, that I should bear witness unto the Truth."

It is our prayer that the twin flames of all sons and daughters of the Father/Mother God evolving in this and every system of worlds likewise fulfill their witness of the Law of Love—by the flame of Mother, through the teaching of the law and the prophets, the community of the Christ and the Buddha, and the path of initiation through the Guru/chela relationship which God in the person of the ascended and unascended masters has also vouchsafed to us in this dispensation.

Cosmic Consciousness can be for you the very first step of your own personal alchemy in the putting on of the garment of the Lord.

As you read page by page the message of love dictated to me by the Messenger of Love, our Ever-Present Guru, won't you enter into the heart of Lanello, our beloved?

Won't you put on the garment
of his self-awareness in God? Won't
you take from him the momentum
of his self-mastery in the cycles of
time and space which he would
give to you as the glad free offering
of his soul's rejoicing "everywhere
in the consciousness of God"?

My beloved, *Cosmic Consciousness*
is the testimony, the teaching, and the
summum bonum of the experience
of one who walked among us,
knew God, and became one with his
everlasting consciousness.

He bids us do the same. He
takes our hand. He shows us the way.

By his love, I AM

Elizabeth Clare Prophet

Meditations
Recommended by Lanello

Call to the Fire Breath
Spoken of by Lanello on page 119

I AM, I AM, I AM the fire breath of God
From the heart of beloved Alpha and Omega.
This day I AM the immaculate concept
In expression everywhere I move.
Now I AM full of joy
For now I AM the full expression
Of divine love.

My beloved I AM Presence,
Seal me now
Within the very heart of
The expanding fire breath of God:
Let its purity, wholeness, and love
Manifest everywhere I AM today and forever!

I accept this done right now with full power.
I AM this done right now with full power.
I AM, I AM, I AM God-life expressing perfection
all ways at all times.

This which I call forth for myself I call forth
for every man, woman, and child on this planet.

An explanation of these dynamic decrees and how they work is given
in the books *The Science of the Spoken Word* and *Prayer and Meditation* by
Mark and Elizabeth Prophet and in *The Science of the Spoken Word*, cassette
album A7736. A complete selection of decrees is available in *Prayers,
Meditations, and Dynamic Decrees for the Coming Revolution in Higher Consciousness*.
Write Summit University Press, Box A, Livingston, Montana 59047.

Balance the Threefold Flame in Me
Spoken of by Lanello in chapter two

In the name of the beloved mighty victorious Presence of God, I AM in me, and my very own beloved Holy Christ Self, I call to the heart of the Saviour Jesus Christ and the servant-sons of God who are with him in heaven—beloved Helios and Vesta and the threefold flame of love, wisdom, and power in the heart of the Great Central Sun, to beloved Morya El, beloved Lanto, beloved Paul the Venetian, beloved mighty Victory, beloved Goddess of Liberty, the seven mighty Elohim, beloved Lanello, the entire Spirit of the Great White Brotherhood and the World Mother, elemental life—fire, air, water, and earth! to balance, blaze, and expand the threefold flame within my heart until I AM manifesting all of thee and naught of the human remains.

Take complete dominion and control over my four lower bodies and raise me and all life by the power of the three-times-three into the glorious resurrection and ascension in the light! In the name of the Father, the Mother, the Son, and the Holy Spirit, I decree:

> Balance the threefold flame in me (3x)
>> Beloved I AM!
> Balance the threefold flame in me (3x)
>> Take thy command!
> Balance the threefold flame in me (3x)
>> Magnify it each hour!
> Balance the threefold flame in me (3x)
>> Love, wisdom, and power!
>
> Use "blaze" then "expand" in place of "balance" the second and third time this decree is given.

And in full faith I consciously accept this manifest, manifest, manifest (3x) right here and now with full power, eternally sustained, all-powerfully active, ever expanding, and world enfolding until all are wholly ascended in the light and free! Beloved I AM, beloved I AM, beloved I AM!

Golden Pink Glow Ray
Spoken of by Lanello on page 166

In the name of the beloved mighty victorious
Presence of God, I AM in me, and my very own beloved
Holy Christ Self, I call to the heart of the Saviour
Jesus Christ and the servant-sons of God who are with
him in heaven—to the heart of beloved Serapis Bey
and the Brotherhood at Luxor, beloved Lord Gautama,
beloved Saint Germain, beloved God and Goddess Meru,
beloved Sanat Kumara and the Holy Kumaras,
the cosmic being Harmony, the seven mighty Elohim,
the seven beloved archangels and their archeiai, the
seven beloved chohans of the rays, beloved Lanello,
the entire Spirit of the Great White Brotherhood and the
World Mother, elemental life—fire, air, water, and earth!

1. I AM calling today for thy golden pink ray
   To manifest round my form.
   Golden pink light, dazzling bright,
   My four lower bodies adorn!

   Refrain:
   O Brotherhood at Luxor and
      blessed Serapis Bey,
   Hear our call and answer
      by love's ascending ray.
   Charge, charge, charge our being
   With essence pure and bright;
   Let thy hallowed radiance
   Of ascension's mighty light
   Blaze its dazzling light rays
   Upward in God's name,
   Till all of heaven claims us
   For God's ascending flame.

2. Saturate me with golden pink light,
   Make my four lower bodies bright;
   Saturate me with ascension's ray,
   Raise my four lower bodies today!

3. Surround us now with golden pink love
   Illumined and charged with light from above;
   Absorbing this with lightning speed,
   I AM fully charged with Victory's mead.

   And in full faith . . .

Notes

For an alphabetical listing of many of the philosophical and hierarchical terms used in *Cosmic Consciousness*, see the comprehensive glossary, "The Alchemy of the Word: Stones for the Wise Masterbuilders," in *Saint Germain On Alchemy*.

foreword

1. Acts 1:11.
2. John 14:12.
3. John 1:9.
4. Rev. 19:7.
5. John 16:7.
6. John 17:11, 21, 22.
7. Matt. 24:27.
8. John 3:6.
9. I Cor. 15:49.
10. Rev. 3:12.
11. John 3:8.
12. II Cor. 3:18.
13. Gen. 3:19.
14. Mal. 4:2.
15. John 14:18, 19.

chapter one

1. I Cor. 15:53.
2. II Pet. 3:10, 12.
3. Prov. 16:25.
4. John 8:32.
5. Matt. 14:15–21.
6. Col. 3:3.
7. **Chohan.** Tibetan for lord or master; a chief. Each of the seven rays has a chohan who focuses the Christ consciousness of the ray. The names of the chohans of the rays are as follows: First ray, El Morya; second ray, Lanto; third ray, Paul the Venetian; fourth ray, Serapis Bey; fifth ray, Hilarion; sixth ray, Nada; seventh ray, Saint Germain. See *Lords of the Seven Rays*, pocketbook, $5.95; *Saint Germain On Alchemy*, pocketbook, pp. 378-79, $5.95.
8. Isa. 30:20.
9. Mary's Scriptural Rosary for the New Age,

dictated by Mother Mary to Elizabeth Clare Prophet,
is published in the cassette album A8048 and in the
book *My Soul Doth Magnify the Lord!* quality paperback, $7.95.
A Child's Rosary to Mother Mary is published in the 3-cassette
albums A7864, A7905, A7934, and A8045, $9.95 each, and
The Fourteenth Rosary: The Mystery of Surrender in the 2-cassette
album V7538, $12.95.
   10. I Cor. 6:19, 20.

chapter two

   1. Rom. 12:1.
   2. For a definition of **Spirit** and **soul**, see pp. 8–9
of *Climb the Highest Mountain*, hardback, $21.95; quality
paperback, $16.95; *Saint Germain On Alchemy*, pp. 452,
453.
   3. With the gift of identity, God gave to man seven
forcefields, each one having a different frequency
and therefore providing a unique opportunity to focus
the individuality of God's consciousness. These seven
forcefields of awareness are: the I AM Presence,
also known as the Electronic Presence of God, which
holds the pattern of the Real Self; the causal body
of man, which surrounds the I AM Presence as the
chalice for all good that the individual has elected to
qualify in word, thought, and deed since the moment
of creation when the blueprint of his identity was
sealed in the fiery core of the God Self; the Christ Self,
focal point for the manifestation of the Universal Christ
within the individual through the action of the
Holy Spirit; and the **four lower bodies:** the etheric or
memory body, vehicle for the soul, holding the
blueprint of the perfect image to be outpictured in
the world of form; the mental body, vehicle for the
mind of God through Christ; the emotional body,
vehicle for God's feelings and energy in motion;
the physical body, vehicle for God's power and focal

point for the crystallization of the energies of the other six bodies in form. The four lower bodies are reference points for man's mastery of himself and his environment through the mastery of the four cosmic forces known as earth, air, fire, and water. See *Saint Germain On Alchemy*, pp. 365-66, 369-70, 372-77, 383-84, 400-401, 410, 426-27, 436.

4. Rom. 8:17.
5. I Cor. 15:41.
6. I Cor. 15:40.
7. John 3:30.
8. Matt. 16:25.

chapter three

1. I Cor. 15:26.
2. Serapis Bey, *Dossier on the Ascension*, quality paperback, $5.95.
3. Mark 15:37-39.
4. William Shakespeare, *Hamlet*, act 3, sc. 1, line 67.
5. Heb. 9:27.
6. Phil. 1:21.
7. Isa. 1:18.
8. Gen. 1:26.
9. John 8:44.
10. Rom. 6:3.
11. I Pet. 1:19.
12. Yet it is our understanding that Jesus voluntarily retained 7 percent of his personal karma as an anchoring point for his mission in order to demonstrate his mastery of the law by the power of his example.
13. John 1:29.
14. Matt. 19:28.
15. Rom. 6:4.
16. Rom. 6:5–7.
17. Matt. 3:11.
18. Rom. 8:7.

19. Rev. 22:11.
20. Matt. 5:18.
21. Rom. 6:8, 9.
22. Rom. 6:10, 11.
23. Rev. 2:11; 20:6, 14; 21:8.
24. Christopher Isherwood, *Ramakrishna and His Disciples* (London: Methuen & Co., 1965), p. 315.
25. John 14:2, 3.
26. Luke 24:49.

chapter four

1. James 4:8.
2. **I AM Presence.** The I AM THAT I AM (Exod. 3:13–15); the individualized Presence of God focused for each individual soul. The God-identity of the individual; the Divine Monad; the individual Source. The origin of the soul focused in the planes of Spirit just above the physical form; the personification of the God flame for the individual. See Chart of Your Divine Self opposite page 33.
3. John 10:16.
4. John 8:58.
5. John 1:9.
6. Phil. 2:10, 11.
7. Gen. 1:27; 5:2.
8. Matt. 12:31, 32.
9. **The Great White Brotherhood.** Fraternity of saints, sages, and ascended masters of all ages who— coming from every nation, race, and religion— have reunited with the Spirit of the living God and who comprise the heavenly hosts. The term "white" refers to the halo of white light that surrounds their forms. The Brotherhood also includes in its ranks certain unascended chelas of the ascended masters. See *The Great White Brotherhood in the Culture, History, and Religion of America,* quality paperback, $10.95; *Saint Germain On Alchemy,* pp. 406-7.

10. For more information on Church Universal and Triumphant, write Box A, Livingston, Montana 59047.

11. Lanello is speaking of the 'inner' Church Universal and Triumphant as the community of the Holy Spirit and the mystical body of God in heaven and on earth. Always and forever it is this Light of the hearts of the faithful in Christ—merged as One and bound to the Faithful and True—which is the ultimate manifestation of the City Foursquare (Rev. 21:16) and not a mere outer organization.

12. I John 2:18, 22.

13. Gen. 3:14, 15; Isa. 14:12; Rev. 12:3, 4, 9, 12–17.

14. Matt. 15:14.

15. Exod. 20:2.

16. Exod. 3:14.

chapter five

1. Deut. 32:35; Rom. 12:19.

2. Mark 4:39.

3. **Records of akasha.** A substance and dimension upon which the recordings of all that has taken place in an individual's world are "written" by recording angels. Akashic records can be read by those whose spiritual faculties are developed. See *Saint Germain On Alchemy*, p. 355.

4. Gen. 4:9.

5. Num. 17:8.

6. I Cor. 3:6.

chapter six

1. Eph. 4:22–24; Col. 3:9, 10.

2. John 19:23.

3. Mark 5:1–20.

4. Gen. 1:26, 28.

5. I Cor. 3:16; II Cor. 6:16.

6. Rom. 7:23.

7. Heb. 11:3.

chapter seven

1. Prov. 17:3.
2. Gen. 1:27; 5:2.
3. John 3:8.
4. I Cor. 15:47, 48.

5. **The Dark Cycle** of the return of mankind's karma began on April 23, 1969. It is a period when mankind's misqualified energy (i.e., their returning negative karma), held in abeyance for centuries under the great mercy of the Law, is released according to the cycles of the initiations of the solar hierarchies for balance in this period of transition into the Aquarian age.

6. Heb. 13:2.
7. Acts 2:2.

chapter eight

1. Luke 10:7.
2. For exercises in the scientific purification of the chakras, see *Intermediate Studies of the Human Aura*, $7.95.
3. Acts 2:3.

chapter nine

1. John 1:14; Luke 2:32.
2. Prov. 9:10.
3. Ezek. 1:4.
4. **Crystal.** Quartz that is transparent or nearly so and that is either colorless or only slightly tinged; a body that is formed by the solidification of a chemical element, a compound, or a mixture and has a regularly repeating internal arrangement of its atoms and often external plane faces. (All solids, however, with minor exceptions, have orderly internal atomic arrangements and so are classed as crystals.)
5. *Studies in Alchemy*, quality paperback, $3.95.

chapter ten

1. Dan. 7:9.

chapter eleven

1. Matt. 22:1–14.
2. Matt. 13:45, 46.

3. For more information on quarterly conferences and retreats, write Box A, Livingston, Montana 59047.

4. The Ascension Temple, retreat of Serapis Bey located in the etheric plane over Luxor, Egypt.

chapter twelve

1. II Kings 2:1–14.
2. John 6:53, 54.
3. Acts 2:1–4.
4. Matt. 3:16, 17.
5. I Cor. 12:3.
6. I Cor. 12:6.
7. I Cor. 12:13.
8. I Cor. 12:8–11.
9. John 4:35.
10. Rev. 22:20.
11. John 10:4.

chapter thirteen

1. On July 6, 1963, following Omri-Tas' dictation, conferees attending the Freedom Class in Washington, D.C., witnessed the physical precipitation of hundreds of violet spheres over the nation's capital.

chapter fourteen

1. Job 42:2–5.
2. Job 42:7–9.
3. **Saturn.** Sign of the tester and the redeemer, practicality and prudence; also called "Seter" or "Satan" signifying evil, loss, and misfortune.
4. Rev. 13:7.
5. Job 1:8.
6. Rev. 11:7.
7. Job 1:11.
8. Job 2:10.
9. Job 2:11-13.
10. Job 3:1-3.
11. Job 3:21.
12. Exod. 3:1.
13. Job 3:25.
14. Matt. 5:26.

Unless otherwise noted, all publications and audiocassettes are Summit University Press (Box A, Livingston, MT 59047), released under the messengership of Mark L. Prophet and Elizabeth Clare Prophet. **Postage for books** $5.95 and under, please add $.50 for the first book, $.25 each additional book; for books $7.95 through $15.95, add $1.00 for the first, $.50 each additional; for books $16.95 and over, add $1.50 for the first, $.75 each additional. **For 2- or 3-cassette albums,** add $.90 for the first album, $.30 for each additional album.

Index of Scripture

SUMMIT UNIVERSITY

I n every age there have been some, the few, who have pursued an understanding of God and of selfhood that transcends the current traditions of doctrine and dogma. Compelled by a faith that knows the freedom To Be, they have sought to expand their awareness of God by probing and proving the infinite expressions of his Law. Through the true science of religion, they have penetrated the mysteries of both Spirit and Matter and come to experience God as the All-in-all.

Having discovered the key to Reality, these sons and daughters of God have gathered disciples who desired to pursue the disciplines of universal Law and the inner teachings of the mystery schools. Thus Jesus chose his apostles, Bodhidharma his monks, and Pythagoras his initiates at Crotona. Gautama Buddha called his disciples to form the *sangha* (community) and King Arthur summoned his knights of the Round Table to the quest for the Holy Grail.

Summit University is Maitreya's Mystery School for men and women of the twentieth century who are searching for the great synthesis—the gnosis of Truth which the teachings of the Ascended Masters afford. These adepts are counted among the few who have overcome in every age to join the immortals as our elder brothers and sisters on the Path.

Gautama Buddha and Lord Maitreya sponsor Summit University with the World Teachers Jesus and Kuthumi, the Lords of the Seven Rays, the Divine Mother, the beloved Archangels and the "numberless numbers" of "saints robed in white" who have graduated from earth's schoolroom and are known collectively as the Great White Brotherhood. To this university of the Spirit they lend their flame, their counsel and the momentum of their attainment, even as they fully give the living Teaching to us who would follow in their footsteps to the Source of that reality which they have become.

Founded in 1971 under the direction of the Messengers Mark L. Prophet and Elizabeth Clare Prophet, Summit University holds three twelve-week retreats each year—fall, winter, and spring quarters—as well as two-week summer and weekend seminars, and five-day quarterly conferences. Each course is based on the development of the threefold flame and the unfoldment of the inner potential of the Christ, the Buddha, and the Mother flame. Through the teachings of the Ascended Masters dictated to the Messengers, students at Summit University pursue the disciplines on the path of the ascension for the soul's ultimate reunion with the Spirit of the living God.

This includes the study of the sacred scriptures of East and West taught by Jesus and Gautama, John the Beloved and other adepts of the Sacred Heart; exercises in the self-mastery of the chakras and the aura under Kuthumi and Djwal Kul; beginning and intermediate studies in alchemy under the Ascended Master Saint Germain; the Cosmic Clock—a new-age astrology for charting the cycles of personal psychology, karma, and initiation diagramed by Mother Mary; the science of the spoken Word combining prayer, meditation, dynamic decrees and visualization—all vital keys to the soul's liberation in the Aquarian age.

In addition to weekend services including lectures and dictations from the Masters delivered through the Messengers (in person or on videotape), a midweek healing service—"Be Thou Made Whole!"—is held in the Chapel of the Holy Grail at which the Messenger or ministers offer invocations for the infirm and the healing of the nations. "Watch with Me" Jesus' Vigil of the Hours is also kept with violet-flame decrees for world transmutation.

Students are taught by professionals in the medical and health fields to put into practice some of the lost arts of healing, including prayer and scientific fasting, realignment through balanced nutrition, and natural alternatives to achieve wholeness on a path whose goal is the return to the Law of the One through the soul's reintegration with the inner blueprint. The psychology of the family, marriage, and meditations for the conception of new-age children are discussed and counseling for service in the world community is available.

Teachings and meditations of the Buddha taught by Lord Gautama, Lord Maitreya, Lanello, and the bodhisattvas of East and West are a highlight of Summit University experience. The violet-flame and bija mantras with those of Buddha and Kuan Yin enhance the raising of the Kundalini under the sponsorship of Saint Germain. Classes in Hatha Yoga convene daily, while spiritual initiations as a transfer of Light from the Ascended Masters through the Messengers are given to each student at healing services and at the conclusion of the quarter.

Summit University is a twelve-week spiral that begins with you as self-awareness and ends with you as God Self-awareness. As you traverse the spiral, light intensifies, darkness is transmuted. Energies are aligned, chakras are cleared, and the soul is poised for the victorious fulfillment of the individual divine plan. And you are experiencing the rebirth day by day as, in the words of the apostle Paul, you "put off the old man" being "renewed in the spirit of your mind" and "put on the new man which after God is created in righteousness and true holiness." (Eph. 4:22–24)

In addition to preparing the student to enter into the Guru/chela relationship with the Ascended Masters and the path of initiation outlined in their retreats, the academic standards of Summit University, with emphasis on the basic skills of both oral and written communication, prepare students to enroll in undergraduate and graduate programs in accredited schools and to pursue careers as constructive members of the international community. A high school diploma (or its equivalent) is required, a working knowledge of the English language, and a willingness to become the disciplined one—the disciple of the Great God Self of all.

Summit University is a college of religion, science and culture, qualifying students of any religious affiliation to deliver the Lost Teachings of Jesus and his prophecy for these troubled times. Advanced levels prepare students for ordination as ministers (ministering servants) in Church Universal and Triumphant. Taking its sponsorship and authority from the Holy Spirit, the saints and God's calling upon the Messengers, Summit University has neither sought nor received regional or national accreditation.

Summit University is a way of life that is an integral part of Camelot—an Aquarian-age community located in the Paradise Valley on the 33,000-acre Royal Teton Ranch in southwest Montana adjacent to Yellowstone Park. Here ancient truths become the joy of everyday living in a circle of fellowship of kindred souls drawn together for the fulfillment of their mission in the Universal Christ through the oneness of the Holy Spirit. The Summit University Service/Study Program offers apprenticeship training in all phases of organic farming and ranching, construction, and related community services as well as publishing—from the spoken to the written Word.

Montessori International is the place prepared at the Royal Teton Ranch for the tutoring of the souls of younger seekers on the Path. A private school for infants through twelfth grade, Montessori International was founded in 1970 by Mark and Elizabeth Prophet. Dedicated to the educational principles set forth by Dr. Maria Montessori, its faculty strives to maintain standards of academic excellence and the true education of the heart for the child's unfoldment of his Inner Self.

For those aspiring to become teachers of children through age seven, Summit University Level II in conjunction with the Pan-American Montessori Society offers, under the capable direction of Dr. Elisabeth Caspari or her personally trained Master Teachers, an in-depth study of the Montessori method and its application at home and in the classroom. This six-month program includes an examination of one's personal psychology, tracing behavioral characteristics from birth through childhood and adolescence to the present, taking into consideration the sequences of karma and reincarnation as well as hereditary and environmental influences in child development. Following their successful completion of this information course, students may apply for acceptance into the one- or two-year internship programs, which upon graduation lead to teacher certification from the Pan-American Montessori Society.

For information on Summit University and related programs or how to contact the center nearest you for group meetings and study materials, including a library of publications and audio- and videocassettes of the teachings of the Ascended Masters, call or write Camelot at the Royal Teton Ranch, Box A, Livingston, MT 59047 (406) 222-8300.

Summit University does not discriminate on the basis of race, color, sex, national or ethnic origin in its admission policies, programs, and activities.

Welcome to the Heart
of the Inner Retreat
The Place of Great Encounters

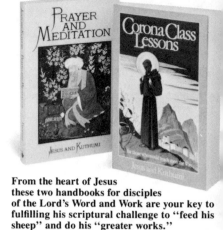

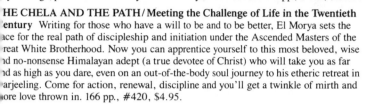

FOR MORE INFORMATION

For information about the Keepers of the Flame fraternity and monthly lessons; dictations of the Ascended Masters published weekly as Pearls of Wisdom; Summit University three-month and weekend retreats; two-week summer seminars and quarterly conferences which convene at the Royal Teton Ranch, a 33,000-acre self-sufficient spiritual community-in-the-making, as well as the Summit University Service/Study Program with apprenticeship in all phases of organic farming, ranching, macrobiotic cooking, construction, publishing and related community services; Montessori International private school, preschool through twelfth grade for children of Keepers of the Flame; and the Ascended Masters' library and study center nearest you, call or write Summit University Press, Box A, Livingston, Montana 59047-1390. Telephone: (406) 222-8300.

Paperback books, audio- and videocassettes on the teachings of the Ascended Masters dictated to their Messengers, Mark L. Prophet and Elizabeth Clare Prophet—including a video series of Ascended Master dictations on "Prophecy in the New Age," a Summit University Forum TV series with Mrs. Prophet interviewing outstanding experts in the field of health and Nature's alternatives to healing, and another on the defense of freedom—are available through Summit University Press. Write for free catalogue and information packet.

Upon your request we are also happy to send you particulars on this summer's international conference at the Royal Teton Ranch—survival seminars, wilderness treks, teachings of Saint Germain, dictations from the Ascended Masters, prophecy on political and social issues, initiation through the Messenger of the Great White Brotherhood, meditation, yoga, the science of the spoken Word, children's program, summer camping and RV accommodations, and homesteading at Glastonbury.

All at the ranch send you our hearts' love and a joyful welcome to the Inner Retreat!

Reach out for the **LIFELINE TO THE PRESENCE.**
Let us pray with you!
To all who are beset by depression, suicide,
difficulties or insurmountable problems, we say
MAKE THE CALL! (406) 848-7441